Lancashire

Dalesman Publishing Company
Stable Courtyard, Broughton Hall,
Skipton, North Yorkshire BD23 3AE

First Edition 1998

Text © John Gillham 1998
Maps by Jeremy Ashcroft
Cover photograph: Pendle Hill by Jacqui
Cordingley

A British Library Cataloguing in Publication
record is available for this book

ISBN 185568 124 2

All rights reserved. This book must not be circulated in any
form of binding or cover other than that in which it is
published and without similar condition of this being
imposed on the subsequent purchaser. No part of this
publication may be reproduced, stored on a retrieval system
or transmitted in any form, or by any means, electronic,
mechanical, photocopying, recording or otherwise, without
either prior permission in writing from the publisher or a
licence permitting restricted copying. In the United
Kingdom such licences are issued by the Copyright
Licensing Agency, 90 Tottenham Court Road, London, W1P
9HE. The right of John Gillham to be identified as author of
this work has been asserted in accordance with Copyright
Designs and Patents Acts 1988.

Printed by Midas Printing (HK) Ltd

Lancashire

John Gillham

Series editor Terry Marsh

DALESMAN

Lancashire

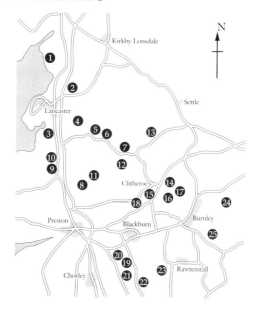

Publisher's Note
The information given in this book has been provided in good faith and is intended only as a general guide. Whilst all reasonable efforts have been made to ensure that details were correct at the time of publication, the author and Dalesman Publishing Company Ltd cannot accept any responsibility for inaccuracies. It is the responsibility of individuals undertaking outdoor activities to approach the activity with caution and, especially if inexperienced, to do so under appropriate supervision. They should also carry the appropriate equipment and maps, be properly clothed and have adequate footwear. The sport described in this book is strenuous and individuals should ensure that they are suitably fit before embarking upon it.

Contents

Introduction

When Lancashire comes to mind, those outside the area could be forgiven for thinking it was just an industrial area between Manchester, Yorkshire, and the mountains of Cumbria. It has after all been coloured for years by images of cloth caps, cricket and clogs; of Lowry landscapes where row upon row of red terraces lead the eye to those dark satanic mills and a rim of misty moorland on the skyline.

And yet Lancashire has some of England's best walking outside the National Parks. Whether you like to stroll by riversides or climb to the hilltops, the Red Rose county has something to offer.

Lancashire is a little smaller these days, both outwards and upwards. Unpopular 1974 boundary changes robbed the county of the Old Man of Coniston, its highest hill at 2,633ft/801m, and handed it, along with the Furness area and Westmorland, to Cumbria. Now Green Hill (2,060ft/628m), near Kirkby Lonsdale, is highest. Although Lancashire has lost some of its finest hills to Cumbria, it has also gained some beautiful country at Yorkshire's expense, the finest being the green rolling countryside east of Bowland and Pendle.

Three great rivers, the Lune, the Wyre and the Ribble, flow through Lancashire to the sea. Though the best Wyre walks are in the upper reaches in Bowland, the Lune and Ribble offer many strolls through idyllic green pastures and woods. A fourth river is as fair as any in England. Being a mere tributary of the Ribble, the Hodder doesn't get the recognition it deserves, but I know of no other river that can claim to be so beautiful and untainted for its entire length.

Those who like to walk on the hilltops are well served, for this is self-proclaimed 'hill country'. Pendle Hill must rank as the most popular of the high places. Synonymous with tales of witchcraft and treachery, this dark escarpment rises in relative isolation from the green fields of the Ribble and the rooftops of East Lancashire.

I have to admit bias at this point, for I started my walking on the fells of Bowland and I am truly besotted with the place. True, it has its honeypots like Parlick and the Trough itself, but explore the inner world of Bowland and you're exploring true wilderness. Evocative names like Wolfhole Crag and Holdron Castle leap out from the map, urging you to replace the mental picture with reality. And reality is no disappointment: heather, dark crags of millstone grit and views, uninterrupted by the trappings of the 20th century, all go to make Bowland a fine place to be.

On the south side of Pendle rising from the towns of Burnley, Nelson and Colne, the South Pennine hills are generally parcelled into smaller sections. Signs of an industrial past still linger here. Derelict mills hide in wooded glens, deep in the folds of the heather moors. Reservoirs, built to supply the mines and canals, bask high on the hillsides, while hamlets surviving from 16th-century farming and weaving communities are dotted along lofty pastured shelves overlooking the valleys. South Pennine walkers can follow old packhorse trails still paved with weathered gritstone; they can look down to the distant mill chimneys of Burnley and Todmorden; they can empathise with the plight of past hill farmers, or they can conjure up characters from a Brontë novel. It's all in a day's walk.

Equipment and Safety

It is extremely important that all walkers are fully equipped and practised in the use of map and compass. Their well-being may depend on it one day.

The Bowland and Pennine uplands can be particularly confusing when mist descends. It is essential to know one's whereabouts at all times, and to know the direction required to get safely down to civilisation.

Make sure to take enough food and water – keep additional emergency rations in the corner of the rucksack. Good waterproofs are essential. Remember, getting cold and wet will render the walker vulnerable to hypothermia, even outside the winter months.

It is important to wear good walking boots on the hills, for shoes have insufficient grip and ankle support on difficult terrain. When snow and ice cover the hills it is more prudent to be equipped with, and know how to use, crampons and an ice-axe. Keep the latter out, once on the slopes, for an ice-axe strapped to a rucksack never saved anyone. It is a good idea to pack some emergency medical supplies (plasters, bandages etc.): there are plenty of good kits available.

Maps

While Jeremy Ashcroft's maps accompanying each walk are beautifully crafted they are not detailed enough for use in the field. Outdoor Leisure and Explorer 1:25,000 maps are best as they show greater detail including the important field boundaries. The double-sided Ordnance Survey Outdoor Leisure maps No 21 'South Pennines', No 41 'Forest of Bowland' and Explorer No 19 'West Pennine Moors' together cover most of the walks in the book, but a few walks in the northern areas need one or more of the Outdoor Leisure No 2 'Yorkshire Dales Western Area' or Landranger No 97 'Kendal and Morecambe' and 102 'Preston and Blackpool'.

Access

The boundaries of the access areas are marked on the OS Outdoor Leisure and Explorer maps with a purple line. Entry and exit points are marked with an arrow. Walkers should remember however that many of the heather moors are managed for grouse shooting and on shooting days, which will occur between August 12 and December 10, and times of high fire risk, the access areas will be closed to the public with the exception of the rights of way.

Caring for the Countryside

With modern methods and increased productivity for the large units, it is becoming much harder for farmers to make a living from the land. Walkers can help by showing consideration for the rural environment, which means shutting gates behind them (except for those that are wedged open), not leaving litter, and by keeping dogs on a lead in sheep country.

Unfortunately, the explosion of people taking to the hills has meant that some footpaths have become eroded. There is not a lot the walker can do (except the unthinkable, staying at home) but they can help in a small way:

Avoid walking in very large groups;

Do not walk along the very edge of the footpath, which makes it wider;

If a cart track has one of those pleasant grass islands through the middle, keep it that way by sticking to the stony bits;

Do not wear heavyweight mountain boots for low-level or moorland paths. Use a lightweight pair if possible;

Walk single file across farming land;

You may have a favourite path, but try not to love it to death. Vary your walks and walking areas;

... and finally, if you take your car, leave it where it doesn't obstruct other road users or the local community – not by farmers' gates or obstructing their tracks.

Useful Addresses

Tourist Information Centres:

Lancaster: 7 Dalton Square, LA1 1PP. Tel: 01524 32878

Preston: The Guild Centre, Lancaster Road, PR1 1HT. Tel: 01772 53731

Blackburn: St George's Hall, BB2 1AA. Tel: 01254 53277

Accrington: Town Hall, Blackburn Road, BB5 1LA. Tel: 01254 386807

Burnley: Burnley Mechanics, Manchester Road, BB11 1JA. Tel: 01282 455485

Nelson: Town Hall, Market Street, BB9 7LG. Tel: 01282 692890

Clitheroe: 12/14 Market Place, BB7 2RA. Tel: 01200 425566

Barnoldswick: The Old Library, Fernlea Avenue, BB8 5DW. Tel:01282 817046

Rawtenstall: 41-45 Kay Street, BB4 7LS. Tel: 01706 226590

The Ramblers' Association: 1-5 Wandsworth Road, London, SW8 2XX. Tel: 0171 582 6878

Transport

The valleys are well served by bus and train, the narrow country lanes in remote rural areas such as Bowland are not well served by bus.

Buses:

On Sundays three bus services link Lancashire towns with Bowland. The 40 runs from Colne and Burnley to Morecambe-Grange (Border). The 44 runs from Preston to Clitheroe via the Trough of Bowland (Stagecoach Ribble). The 45 links Darwen and Blackburn with Slaidburn.

Lancashire County Council has produced a leaflet and timetable on the Bowland Pathfinder service. It should be available at Tourist Information Centres (see above).

Bus companies:

Border: Tel: 01282 456351

Stagecoach: Tel: 01772 886633

Blackburn Transport: Tel: 01254 51112

Bus Stations:

Blackburn: Tel: 01254 681120

Burnley: Tel: 01282 423125

Clitheroe: Tel: 01200 442226

Lancaster: Tel: 01524 841656

Preston: 01772 556618

The main railway lines are:

London Euston to Glasgow, serving Preston Lancaster, Carnforth;

A branch line to Barrow serves Arnside and Silverdale;

A branch line to Clitheroe is helpful for Bowland;

A line runs from Preston to Colne via Blackburn, Accrington, Burnley and Nelson;

A branch line from Blackburn calls at Darwen and Entwistle for the West Pennine Moors;

The Preston to Manchester trains call at Chorley, Adlington and Blackrod for the Anglezarke, Winter Hill area.

For train information: Tel: 0345 484950

North of the County

Before 1974 the north of the county would have included Barrow, Walney Island and some of the Coniston Fells. Unfortunately for Lancashire, these outposts were gifted, along with the whole of Westmorland, to Cumbria. Today, the county spreads little further than Lancaster.

The Arnside/Silverdale Area of Outstanding Natural Beauty also straddles the borders, the former being in Cumbria: the latter in Lancashire. Here, the limestone stratum of the Yorkshire Dales meets the sea at Morecambe Bay. Ivory knolls, cloaked with richly diverse woodland, overlook Leighton Moss Nature Reserve on one side and coastal salt marshes on the other. Nature lovers will be enthralled by the bird and plant-life.

The Lune must be one of the most scenic rivers in England. The exquisite views from the Crook o' Lune near Caton have been noted by poets Wordsworth and Thomas Gray. Many footpaths trace the Lune's banks; both through the historical city of Lancaster and along its meandering course through pastoral countryside. Looking across its peaceful waters to the purple heathered hills of Bowland and the impressive tiered summit of Ingleborough you will be delighted that you came.

erdale and
n Moss

Silverdale sits between wooded limestone hills bordering the salt marshes of the Kent Estuary and looks out across Morecambe Bay to the Lakes. It's a popular place for both walking and bird-watching owing to the varied habitats of woodland, pasture and coast. This circular walk takes a look at all those habitats, including the Leighton Moss and Gait Barrows nature reserves, before exploring the cliffs and marshes of the coast.

Distance:
8½ miles/14km
Height gain: 180ft/55m
Walking time: 5 hours
Type of walk: A varied walk that follows paths and tracks through woods, over limestone, and along coastal marshes and cliffs. There are rough and muddy sections south of Silverdale.
Start/Finish: Leighton Moss, near Silverdale Railway Station. GR476750.
Map: OS Landranger 97: Kendal to Morecambe.

Cautionary note: *Before setting out on this walk, check the tide timetable, which can be bought in local shops, for it's easy to get caught out. Don't wander far from the shore: besides the danger of being stranded by rushing tides, there is dangerous quicksand. If the times are inconvenient, try starting from Silverdale, rather than Leighton Moss.*

Turn left along the lane from the car park, passing the Leighton Moss visitor centre (well worth a visit), then right on the cart track across the Leighton Moss Nature Reserve. The track heads south-east, surrounded by tall bull rushes that sway with the breeze.

Although most hides are for the use of permit holders and RSPB members, the trackside ones are for public viewing of the many birds that occur here, including mallard, teal, coot, tern, and an occasional osprey. The observant may also get to see heron, greylag goose, peregrine, sparrowhawk or the bittern, a rare bird that breeds here.

Beyond the moss the track veers left to pass the farm at Grizedale. Here it becomes a metalled lane skirting woodland and pasture towards Leighton Hall.

A signpost 'to Yealand Storrs' at north-west of the hall highlights a rutted track that takes the route north across rolling pastureland with the wood-cloaked limestone escarpments of Gait Barrows prominent in the view ahead.

After about a half mile, go through the right of two five-bar gates, now keeping the hedge on the left. Ignore the rutted track on the left to Brow Foot Farm, but continue by the hedge until a raised grassy causeway leads the route through the last field before passing to the right of a roadside cottage in the hamlet of Yealand Storrs.

Turn left along the Silverdale road to its first

junction (GR494761). Beyond a five-bar gate a wide westbound track forages through woodland where yew, oak, holly and hawthorn co-exist among limestone outcrops.

Keep to the main track until it veers right uphill. Abandon it now for a path that maintains direction through bracken and scrub.

Watch out for a gap stile by a gate on the left (GR485765), for it marks the start of a cross-field path through the grounds of Gait Barrows Nature Reserve. A group of Exmoor ponies often graze here. Signs claim that this pony is more rare than the giant panda.

The path re-enters woodland near the shores of Hawes Water, a small lake surrounded by squat limestone crags. Turn right along the path following the shoreline, making sure to turn left along the bridleway by the western shore to the lane near Challon Hall.

Turn left along the lane then right on an enclosed footpath descending to another lane. Staggered to the left, the footpath to be followed crosses the railway (take care) before passing between a caravan site and garden centre into Eaves Wood.

There are far more paths in Eaves Wood than are shown on the map. The right of way used on this occasion is the most distinctive one, heading generally west through trees that include yew, lime, oak and beech. In the later stages the path overlooks the fields of Elmslack before coming to a

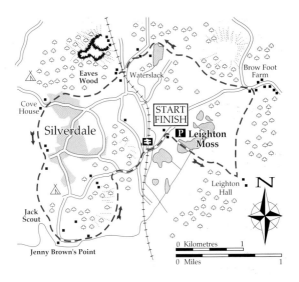

cluster of houses at the northern extremity of Silverdale.

Turn left along the lane, descending to turn right along Cove Road. At a sharp right-hand bend follow the cul-de-sac 'to the Shore'.

If there are any doubts about the tide, use the signposted field paths south into Silverdale, returning to Leighton Hall either by Heald Brow (see walk 2) or by the lanes. Otherwise, proceed along the shoreline salt marshes, which are divided by dykes and pools. Grange-over-Sands languishes beneath squat hills across the marshes and the sands of the Kent Estuary.

Beyond Silverdale the route hugs squat cliffs

beneath Know Hill. On nearing Jack Scout the shoreline becomes rough with mud-caked boulders, and it is easier to scramble up to a narrow eroded path that undulates on grassland at the top of the cliffs.

The path eventually sidles down into a limestone ravine by Jack Scout. Here, the cliffs become higher, and climbers often practise their skills. Go over a stile to the left, then turn right to the other side of the ravine, where the path clambers over rock and through scrub to the top of the cliffs. Walkers will need to exercise care and use their hands on one easy rock section.

A good path now keeps a barbed-wire fence to the right, and continues above the cliffs towards the small jetty at Jenny Brown's Point, where views extend to Fleetwood and the Fylde Coast.

J J Thomlinson

Leighton Hall

A 19th-century scheme to reclaim the marshes between Jenny Brown's Point and Hest Bank ended in failure. Funds were exhausted and the incomplete stony causeway abandoned, later to be submerged by tide-driven sand. Only recently has the Kent's shifting tidal water removed the sand to reveal the old project.

Just short of a small bouldery inlet, the path goes left to meet a lane by an old quarry that was used for the causeway. Follow the lane to its terminus at Jenny Brown's Cottages.

Keep right of the house before following the path along the shore to a crumbling stone chimney, the remains of a copper-smelting works. Continue along more coastal mosses, crossing a stile on the way to a grassy storm embankment that protects Leighton Moss. This is a popular place for widgeon.

At a crossroads of paths by the storm embankment, go straight ahead on a pleasant path beneath Heald Brow. It climbs through very pleasant woodland to meet the road south of Silverdale Green.

Turn right along the road, then right at the next junction, and straight on at the next before coming to the Leighton Moss car park once more.

2 Crook o' Lune and the Lancaster Canal

The Lune, from its source near the much-loved Howgills to its estuary at Morecambe Bay, is one of the North's finest rivers, and at Crook o' Lune it's at its most scenic. This circular walk follows the river westwards towards Lancaster, then at a huge aqueduct climbs to the Lancaster Canal. The canal towpath conveys the route north, from town to country before heading back to the start across fields, lanes and again by the river.

Distance: 8½ miles/14km	**Start/Finish:** Car Park, Crook o' Lune, Nr Caton. GR522648
Height gain: 290ft/90m	**Map:** OS Landranger 97: Kendal to Morecambe, or Outdoor Leisure 41: Forest of Bowland.
Walking time: 4-5 hours	
Type of walk: Easy waterside walk, except for those steps up to the aqueduct.	

The perfect rural riverscape that so impressed romantic poets William Wordsworth and Thomas Gray is still intact at Crook o' Lune. Here, the wide and powerful river forms a graceful U-bend, looping beneath green hillsides, woods and pastures.

Some steps lead from near the entrance of the car park down to the east of two railway bridges.

Don't cross the bridge here, but turn right along the trackbed, now a grassy path. After a short way it crosses the Lune on the western bridge. At its far side, turn right on a footpath signposted as the Lune Riverside Walk. It descends to the riverbank in a series of steps.

The Lune is wide and tree-enshrouded hereabouts, and bends left, while the path threads through the trees, dodging tangled roots near the water's edge. Pleasant green fields replace the trees for a while, but the scenery reverts to woodland and scrub as the path draws close to the old railway line.

As the village of Halton appears high above the far banks, the path becomes more sketchy. In order to avoid dangerously slippery rocks, take some steps on the left to join the railway trackbed again. The riverside path can be regained downstream at some more steps, but don't be tempted by a muddy path that returns to those rocks. It's worth staying with the railway route, however, to see the old Halton railway station whose Victorian canopy and platform are still in good order.

Beyond the bridge linking the station with the village, the route turns right to rejoin the riverside walk. On the far banks are some fine cottages, St Wilfred's church, and a splendid weeping willow. But there's a faint rumble in the distance to disturb this peaceful scene.

The motorway bridge appears and the drone gets louder. The path tucks under it, then crosses a field, before finally giving up the ghost and joining the railway trackbed. By now a five-arched bridge has come into view. After passing mills, factories and the Forte Trust House Motel, the path is pleased to see it.

The bridge turns out to be an aqueduct conveying the Lancaster Canal 221yds/m over the Lune, which flows 21ft/7m below. It's a magnificent piece of 19th-century engineering by John Rennie.

After passing under the aqueduct follow the signposted path to the left, and climb numerous steps to the top. The canal towpath crosses the aqueduct high above the river before taking the route past the houses of Beaumont and into the country. The houses of Morecambe span the skyline beyond the green fields and the London to Glasgow railway line.

Leave the canal at bridge number 115 (GR467653) south-west of Slyne village. A stile in the hedge on the left allows entry onto a cart track that crosses the bridge before heading east. The track, which becomes a pleasant grassy one enclosed by hedges, leads to a metalled access lane to Brantholme, which in turn leads to Hasty Brow Road.

Turn left along the road then straight ahead at the crossroads past the bungalows and houses of Throstle Grove. Turn left along the A6 through the village centre, passing, unless a thirst intervenes, the Cross Keys and the Slyne Lodge public houses.

A right turn at the far end of the village down Bottomdale Road takes the route past the village

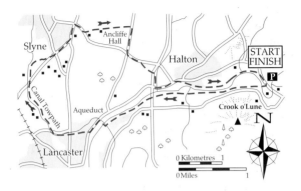

cemetery. Turn left beyond it to go through a kissing gate and east across the sports ground. After crossing two more stiles, the path threads through newly-planted woodland, then across another field to Ancliffe Lane.

Immediately across the road follow the access track towards Ancliffe Hall. A waymarking arrow near the hall shows where the route leaves the track. The path, staggered to the left, continues across fields with a hedge on the right.

Turn right on reaching Kellet Lane, then left at the crossroads. The lane descends to cross the M6 motorway. Someone has erected a seat for those who would like to study this noisy alleyway to the cities.

The best part of Halton village can be viewed by leaving the lane at the cul-de-sac on the right (signposted to Halton Cemetery). By the cemetery a narrow grassy path, passing close enough to the

25

motorway to feel the breeze off the cars and lorries, descends to the bottom road, which passes the splendid square-towered church of St Wilfred's, the White Lion pub and several interesting stone-built cottages. Take the lower road to the right at the crossroads, passing the Greyhound pub before turning right on Station Road, which goes down to the River Lune.

Rather than crossing the bridge, turn left along the stony track passing several depots and mills. The path squeezes through a gap to the right of some unsightly iron gates and continues along the track above the remains of a demolished mill.

Ignore the path down to the river just beyond the mill, for this will necessitate a scramble up muddy banks to rejoin the higher route. The better route stays high and joins the river just past the weir. The scruffiness of the last half mile has now been left behind and the path traverses fields by the riverside before entering woodland where in spring garlic and bluebells form a thick carpet.

The path climbs to the road just short of the Crook o' Lune car park, but a new footpath running parallel to the road saves any walking on tarmac.

3 Glasson and Cockersand Abbey

On the banks of the Lune, not far from Lancaster's bustling streets, the little port of Glasson has known busier days. It's now largely a place for tourists and those seeking leisure on boats. There's good walking here though. This route, which stays close to the coastal marshes, gives lovely views across Morecambe Bay and to the fells of Bowland on its way to Cockersand Abbey, a forlorn seashore ruin.

Distance:
7½ miles/12km
Height gain: 50ft/15m
Walking time: 4 hours
Type of walk: Easy and flat on farm and coastal tracks and field paths
Start/Finish: Car park/picnic site, Conder Green. GR457562
Map: OS Landranger

102: Preston and Blackpool.
Notes: Exceptionally high tides could curtail the walk around Bank End Farm. Check the timetables before setting out. Also, do not wander off the path for there are dangerous quicksands.

Glasson's dock was constructed in 1787 and enabled ships to avoid sailing down the estuary to Lancaster and the tidal problems that entailed. A canal was built to link with the Lancaster canal and a railway to the city added. The railway closed in 1964 but fortunately its trackbed is intact and will be used on the initial stages of this walk.

Turn left out of the car park onto the trackbed to cross the bridge over the mouth of the River Cinder. The track, now lined by hawthorn, gorse and bramble, curves westwards at the edge of the Lune coastal marshes with the houses and cranes of Glasson Dock in the mid-distance.

On entering Glasson, a footpath signpost directs the walk to the road by the Victoria Inn's car park. Across the road the canal enters the dock, now packed with modern yachts, whose tall masts can be seen for many miles.

Turn left over the swing bridge across a lock, then follow the road, Tithebarne Hill, to a T-junction south of the village (GR443556). On the right, a metalled, hedge-lined bridleway, Marsh Lane, takes the route west past a caravan site. Beyond the site the track turns into a muddy one for a short way before fading to a rutted Landrover track across fields.

At Crook Farm the route meets the coast and bracing inshore breezes fill the air with the aroma of seaweed. Across the marshes and the Lune Estuary are the houses of Sunderland with Heysham power station behind.

Turn left along the stony coastal track past Crook Cottage and the Plover Scar lighthouse, near which the track ends. Go through a kissing gate and continue by the coast to the remains of Cockersand Abbey.

The Abbey was built in 1180AD, but after being surrendered to the Kings' Commissioners in 1539, it has

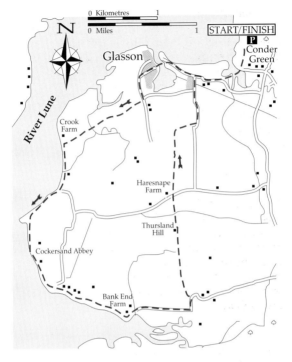

been laid to ruins. Although now surrounded by fields, the abbey would, in those days, have been on an island of clay amid the coastal marshes, as would many of the nearby farms.

From the abbey, return to the coastal path, following it past the Cockerham Sands Country Park caravan site, then onwards past another site at Bank End Farm. Here, a metalled lane heads inland along the edge of Cockerham Marsh. The road swings north. At the apex of a second bend

29

(GR449530), leave it for a hedge-lined farm track on the left, then turn right (north) along another track. To the right the whitewashed Norbreck Farm is beautifully sited on the area's highest hill (75ft/23m).

Beyond a gate the track ceases. Maintain a northbound direction across fields passing to the left of a farm at Thursland Hill. Beyond the farmhouse a clear path veers left with the hedge to go over a stile. Turn right over another stile and continue northwards across more fields, keeping a hedge to the right.

The path reaches a country lane east of Haresnape Farm. Across the road, left of an old shed and through two gates the northbound path continues across yet more pastureland. Keep the fence to the left to pass a derelict farm building. Keep north through a gate, ignoring a footbridge on the right (this belongs to the path bound for Lower Thurnham).

At GR447551, turn right along a cart track that has joined the route from the left. Once through the gate at its terminus, the field boundaries on the left swing right to lead the path to a country lane just half a mile south of Glasson.

By now the masts of the yachts and houses around the docks are in full view. Follow the road north, going straight ahead at the junction to cross the canal. On meeting the B-road, cross it, then follow the old railway track of the outbound route back to the car park at Conder Green.

Bowland, Pendle and The Ribble Valley

Lying between the plains of the Fylde and the valleys of Ribble and Wenning, the Forest of Bowland has been designated an Area of Outstanding Natural Beauty. It is a fascinating mix of pastoral valleys, charming villages surrounded by high heather moors and lower limestone hills.

Bowland has that unspoiled, remote feel. You may have to walk a bit further for that splendid crag, but somehow it doesn't seem to matter: a single dew-glistening bloom looks finer in the meadow than do a score of roses in the florist's shop.

In 1996 agreements between Lancashire County Council and various landowners provided increased access to Bowland's grouse moors, and the situation has been further eased by North West Water's tolerant attitude to *bona fide* walkers. The company allows access to all lands provided that it does not interfere with local land management. In practice this would probably mean exclusion on shooting days (between August 12 and December 10), and at times of high fire risk.

The River Ribble meanders from the urban sprawl of Preston, to cut a wide green swath between the hills of Bowland and Pendle, through the heart of Lancashire.

Many paths trace its riverbanks, allowing

fascinating circular walks linking historic places such as Clitheroe Castle and Whalley Abbey; Stoneyhurst and Ribchester.

Rising above the plains of the Ribble Valley and industrial East Lancashire, Pendle Hill resembles a colossal upturned ship. Synonymous with tales of witchcraft and treachery, it seems to reflect the mood of the heavens. When inky clouds hang low or spill down the hillslopes, it has a sullen aura, yet when the sun shines, it is green, amiable and at peace with the world.

Many miles separate Pendle from its neighbouring hills, allowing views as wide as any in the county. Maybe for this reason it has become Lancashire's favourite hill. But, even on this popular hill, some of the routes, like the ones from Downham and Sabden, are neglected for those on the Big End and along the spine from The Nick of Pendle.

Donald Dakeyne

Downham

4 Ward's Stone From Tower Lodge

Ward's Stone, Bowland's highest fell, will be known to many travellers heading north on the M6 to Scotland or the Lakes. It's that big heather hill seen on the right on the approach to Lancaster: the one with a few rocks on the top. To get a legal circular route to Ward's Stone is impossible without going great distances, or treading a little tarmac. This route, a variation of the classic route, falls somewhere between the two. But Ward's Stone is a fine hill well worth a little collar work.

Distance:
14 miles/23km
Height gain:
1,935ft/590m
Walking time: 8-9 hours
Type of walk: A long, hard walk on paths and tracks, across peat mosses and tracts of heather, followed by a return on country lanes and field paths.

Start/Finish: Tower Lodge. GR604539.
Map: OS Outdoor Leisure 41: Forest of Bowland.
Access: The route uses an agreed access strip and concessionary paths that can be closed on shooting days between August 12 and December 10 and also at times of high fire risk.

The most rewarding ascent of Ward's Stone can be made from Tower Lodge on the 'Trough of Bowland' road. This unusual route involves an extra 500ft/150m of ascent and adds 3 miles/5km to the more traditional route from Tarnbrook. On a fine day the views from the top of White Moor towards Ward's Stone will more than make up for the extra effort.

There is space for a few cars on roadside verges near Tower Lodge at the start of the walk. The ivy-clad dwelling stands in a glen between the bare fellsides of Blaze Moss and White Moor. Tall Scots pines line the shallow Marshaw Wyre, which flows over a rocky bed close to the road.

The northbound track by the side of the lodge has mixed woodland to the left and climbs towards White Moor. Beyond the conifers of the Tower Plantation the track ceases to be a right of way but is one of the new concessionary paths negotiated in 1996. It continues north to the edge of the open moor before turning left beyond a ladder stile in an intake wall.

From here, Tarnbrook Fell, the southern face of Ward's Stone, boasts its shapely, bouldered face, mottled with bracken, heather and bilberry. Below it, the Tarnbrook Wyre cuts a furrow through the hillsides – green, wide and pastured to the west, but heathery in its upper reaches. Above the ravine, the wide shooters' track that the route will later follow can be seen climbing amongst the heather to the skyline.

Beyond the next ladder stile at GR598547 turn right downhill past Harry Wood to Speight Clough

Farm. After passing between the buildings of Spreight Clough, follow the rutted cart track towards Gilberton Farm. Turn right before the farmhouse to cross a wooden footbridge spanning the Tarnbrook Wyre then turn left to follow an access road leading to the Ward's Stone track, sighted earlier.

Turn right along the stony track climbing steadily across the slopes of Tarnbrook Fell to enter an expansive, uncluttered landscape of rough heathland. The stony track ends by some ruins overlooking the infant Wyre, which foams and splashes through its dark, craggy ravine.

The route, now a narrower path, crosses the river

just beyond a small waterfall and, guided by the odd waymarking post, heads north-east across mosses and heather moor to the ridge fence at Brown Syke (GR618583). Views have opened up across Ribblesdale to include the unmistakable outlines of Yorkshire's Three Peaks.

The track along the ridge appears circuitous, but do not be tempted to make a beeline across the marshy bowl of Hare Syke to the summit of Ward's Stone: the ghastly peat groughs and ankle-twisting heathery terrain will make sure that nothing can be gained from this. In contrast, the bare peat found on parts of the correct route is rarely troublesome.

A couple of hundred yards short of the eastern summit of Ward's Stone, the ridge fence deserts the route, choosing instead to double-back and descend Mallowdale Fell. The path maintains direction to the Grey Mare and Foal rocks that mark the eastern summit.

The more famous west summit, which houses the huge boulder from which the hill took its name, is about a third of a mile distant over fairly firm ground. It is worth visiting for the superior views of Morecambe Bay and the Lakeland peaks.

The path, now aiming for Grit Fell, descends westwards among sparse rock to traverse a wide ridge interspersed with peat-hag, mosses, a little heather and moor grasses. Markers remind walkers that the moors are out of bounds outside the narrow access strip as the route crosses a wide 'private' shooters' track which straddles the hill on its way from Abbeystead to Littledale. After climbing a little to Grit Fell's summit, the path comes to a stile in a fence. Once across it turn left descending by the fence, past a tall cairn, the Shooters' Pile, to the road by the Jubilee Tower.

There are ways to reduce the time spent on tarmac but at this stage it may be better to grin and bear it. This route combines the speed of the road with a riverside footpath, without messing about route-finding through farms and farmyards.

Turn left along the road, then follow the right fork down to the pretty village of Abbeystead. On crossing the River Tarnbrook Wyre at Stoops Bridge, take the gated road to the right then almost immediately go through the gate on the left. The path heads east down to cross the Marshaw Wyre on a footbridge.

Across the bridge the path goes left, roughly parallel to the river, passing several woodland copses and scaling several stiles en route to the wooden footbridge at GR578541. Go through the wooden gate in the wall opposite and climb westwards before rejoining the riverbank and squeezing between it and woodland to the left.

The river meanders away from the path, which follows the southern edge of the woods before veering slightly left across the fields to meet the road north of Well Brook Farm. A wall to the right acts as a guide in the final stages. Turn right along the road past Marshaw Farm and by the river back to the start at Tower Lodge.

5 Brennand Great Hill and Wolfhole Crag

One of a handful of new concessionary routes, this is also one of Bowland's best, taking the walker to places with strange sounding, romantic names. Wolfhole Crag lives up to its name: it's a wilderness of a place with mood swings to suit the weather. Millers House and Brennand Great Hill have good rocks and give the Brennand Valley new perspective.

Distance:
9 miles/15km
Height gain:
1,150ft/350m
Walking time: 5/6 hours
Type of walk: A rough moorland walk.
Start/Finish: Tower Lodge. GR604539.

Map: OS Outdoor Leisure 41: Forest of Bowland.
Access: The route uses concessionary paths that can be closed on shooting days between August 12 and December 10 and at times of high fire risk.

The walk begins at the ivy-clad Tower Lodge, which is beautifully situated by the chattering Marshaw Wyre. There is space for a few cars beneath the tall Scots pines that tower above roadside verges.

A stile to the left of the lodge gives access to a stony track that climbs past some chicken sheds and mixed woodland to the fellside. Beyond the strip of conifers of the Tower Plantation, the track ceases to be a right of way but is one of the new concessionary paths negotiated in 1996. On reaching its termination at the edge of White Moor, scale the ladder stile and turn right to trace the intake wall across moorland.

After passing some gaunt trees, all that remains of the High Tower Plantation, the path turns north-east at a guide post. It climbs towards some wind-blown larches and a ragged, broken wall on the bouldered escarpment of Rowantree Rocks. The path follows the old wall for a while, sticking to the short grass on the escarpment's edge.

There are good views from there to the Trough, where a lonely little road snakes between the whaleback hills of Blaze Moss and Whin Fell.

Another guide post points the way of the route, which diverts from the wall on a trackless course north-east towards the craggy tor of Millers House. The best course sticks to the grass and sparse heather at the edge of the tussocky moorland.

At Millers House a tall ridge wall bisects the grassy spur climbing to the rocks on the summit of Brennand Great Hill. Land to the east falls away to the upper Brennand Valley, a scything and lonely tributary of the Whitendale River. At its head extensive flanks of boulder-clad moss rise to Wolfhole Crag.

Most of the surrounding hills rise from their valleys like beached whales; especially so if hazy sunlight lends them a silvery hue. But Wolfhole Crag is a dragon. All the slippery curves are gone – replaced by dark, menacing serrated gritstone.

Climb north up the moor to Brennand Great Hill, which turns out to be little more than a spur thrown out from the Ward's Stone-White Hill ridge. To the west of the path there are some good rocks for lunch or a coffee break with a view – that of the upper Wyre valley.

Beyond Brennand Great Hill the route climbs further across the Woodyards. The wall has changed to a fence allowing wide views across the heather, which most of the year gives out a dark and sombre aura. In August, however, the air will be sweet-scented, and the heather a carpet of vivid purple-pink. In spring the peace of the scene will be destroyed by tens of thousands of gulls who flock here to breed. They're a noisy and cunning bunch and you may need a hat.

On reaching the ridge, turn right over the ladder stile and follow a ridge wall to the boulders and trig point on Wolfhole Crag's summit.

To the north, heathered slopes decline to the River Roeburn. The ancient Hornby Road (Salter Fell track), descends the moorland valley with fellsides beyond climbing to White Hill, a big grassy dome and Bowland's second highest hill. Pride of place lies beyond, where the limestone peaks of Ingleborough, Whernside and Pen-y-Ghent stretch across the horizon, proud and distinguished above the fields of Ribblesdale.

From Wolfhole Crag, turn back to head west along

the peaty ridge to the stile, but, rather than returning to Brennand Great Hill, follow the fence along the ridge towards Ward's Stone.

Watch out for the marker poles at Brown Syke: they highlight the route of descent on the narrow path descending south-west across peat and heather down to the River Tarnbrook Wyre.

Not long after the meeting, the Wyre cascades over gritstone slabs in a heather-cloaked ravine. After fording it just above the main falls, the path soon joins a wide shooters' track that tucks under the stony sides of Long Crag before crossing the lower heather slopes of Tarnbrook Fell.

Leave the track just short of Tarnbrook hamlet, to double back left on the access road to Gilberton Farm. Cross the River Wyre on the little wooden footbridge to the left of the vehicle bridge, thus avoiding the farmhouse. This should be followed by a left turn on the track climbing to Spreight Clough Farm.

Go through the farmyard to a gate on the right. Beyond the gate turn left uphill on a sunken grassy track passing to the west of Harry Wood. There are two ladder stiles on the left above the wood, and both are usable on the route back to Tower Lodge. The first is the start of a concessionary path, but the right of way is described from the second as it gives better views when walked in this direction.

Beyond the stile it climbs diagonally across two fields, with ladder stiles in the intervening walls always visible. Take one last look at the craggy southern face of Ward's Stone across the Tarnbrook Wyre valley, then descend a rough pasture, past some derelict air raid shelters to the Tower Lodge track used on the outward route. Descend further to that other Wyre valley – the Marshaw Wyre.

6 Whin Fell and Brennand

Seeing the roadside picnickers on a Sunday afternoon trip through the Trough of Bowland, a visitor could be forgiven for thinking that this was a rather overrated tourist trap – pretty but nothing special. And yet just over that hill to the north, there's a valley with no people in it, except those who live on its farm. The hill is Whin Fell: the valley is Brennand, and the walk is superb.

Distance: 7½ miles/12km	farm lanes in the lonely Brennand and Whitendale valleys.
Height gain: 870ft/265m	
Walking time: 4½ hours	**Start/Finish:** Car park, Dunsop Bridge. GR661501.
Type of walk: A moderate walk straddling high moors but using some tarmac	**Map:** OS Outdoor Leisure 41: Forest of Bowland.

Little Dunsop Bridge occupies a pastured plain close to the meeting of three watercourses, the Hodder, Whitendale and Langden Brook. Once part of the ancient hamlet of Beatrix, the village grew in importance with the coming of the turnpike road through the Trough, and the lead mining at Whitendale, Brennand and Sykes in the 19th century. Today, it's a useful starting point for walks.

From the car park follow the road west over the one-arched stone bridge spanning the River Dunsop before turning right at the T-junction on a lane following a course parallel to Langden Brook.

As the hills close in leave the lane for the Hareden water works road, which descends to cross Langden Brook on a concrete bridge. Through a five-bar gate on the right, cross Hareden Brook on a stone bridge, before turning right by a wall to a stile by the banks of the Langden Brook.

The 1996 OS Outdoor Leisure map has the route crossing the adjacent field, but in reality the path follows the watercourse round the perimeter of the field to cross a stile into open country. Here a well-defined grassy track heads north-west, parallel to the river. Across the valley in Smelt Mill clough, there's a pleasant waterfall, which can look spectacular after rain.

Beyond a rickety footbridge over Langden Brook (GR632511), the path goes through a strip plantation of larches, over a step-stile, then turns right on the Langden waterworks' drive to the Trough road.

Turn left along the road, passing Sykes Farm to Trough Barn, where a footpath signpost by gate and stile points the way along a rutted track. The track winds and climbs by Rams Clough at first, then across rough pastures between the steep grassy flanks of Whins Brow and Sykes Nab.

Once past some woods it gradually assumes a

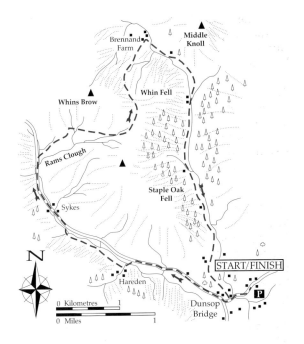

north-east course to the ruins of Trough House. A track, beginning beyond the gate at the far end of the farmyard, heads east beneath Whins Brow. As the route becomes rather sketchy, maintain the easterly direction to a gate by a wall corner at the head of Rams Clough. After crossing the clough beyond the gate, the route swings right then left past the clough tops.

A north-north-east course brings the route to a gate in the ridge fence about 800yds/m east of Whin Fell's summit trig point.

The path from the ridge is waymarked and continues to a cairn overlooking Hind Clough and the Brennand Valley – a view that is one of Bowland's best. Brennand Farm lies far below amid emerald fields that break up the stark wilderness of the surrounding fells. Folds of moorland lead the eye across Bowland's highest peaks, Ward's Stone and White Hill, to the distinctive tops of Yorkshire's Three Peaks, which just manage to peep over their shoulders.

A narrow path known as Ouster Rake descends north-west across the slopes beneath Brennand Stones to a wall corner in Brennand's top pasture. From here it descends further across fields, keeping east of Higher Laithe (barn) and on the left side of Brennand Farm.

Beyond the farmyard, turn right on a lane that follows, then crosses the Brennand River on its way to Lower Brennand Farm. It continues beneath Middle Knoll, a low but bold conical peak. Where the road meets the one from Whitendale Farm, take the right fork, descending south to the Whitendale River.

The Whitendale and Brennand Rivers join forces to become the River Dunsop. The little lane crosses the new river before heading south down the length of the valley past the inky conifers and bracken that cloak the precipitous sides of Beatrix and Staple Oak Fells. Beyond the woods lies Dunsop Bridge and the end of the walk.

7 Dunsop Fell and Whitendale

Some of the Forest of Bowland's finest places lie hidden in the heartlands. Whitendale and Croasdale are two such places where, tentatively, their emerald pastures recede into the dusky shadows of crag-fringed moorland. This fine circular route visits both, and illustrates the superb diversity of Lancashire's countryside.

Distance:
7½ miles/12km
Height gain:
1,870ft/570m
Walking time: 4 hours
Type of walk: Moderate walk across rough, peaty moorland tracks that could be marshy after periods of rain. Boots and map reading skills are essential.
Start/Finish: Slaidburn car park. GR713523.
Map: OS Outdoor Leisure 41: Forest of Bowland.

Leave Slaidburn on the road past the war memorial and north across the bridge over Croasdale Brook. A footpath on the left, halfway up the hill, climbs northwards across fields, and over the crests of two small hills. From the second Croasdale Brook can be seen meandering among pastures before cutting itself a fine, twisting valley in the moors ahead.

The path descends to the banks of the brook before heading for Shay House Farm. On meeting a farm track turn left past the farmhouse. Once across the brook the track climbs out of the valley to the metalled Wood House Lane. Turn right here and follow the lane to a gate at its terminus on Low Fell. Here, the unclassified Hornby Road begins.

Turn left beyond the gate on a rutted track that doubles back to climb the grassy moorland slopes of Dunsop Fell overlooking the cavernous moorland hollow cut by Dunsop Brook. Keeping to the south of the peat hags of Proctor Moss, the track degenerates into a sketchy path, but it's marked by well-spaced posts leading to a gate in the ridge wall at Dunsop Head.

Looking back, Stocks Reservoir lies surrounded by spruce woods, while Pendle Hill rises from the fields of the Ribble Valley.

Beyond the gate a well-defined path descends west-north-west towards Whitendale. It has now become a narrow peaty path cutting through a carpet of heather, and its course has been confirmed by stone cairns and tall waymarking posts.

The scenes are dominated by two rock-studded hills, Whin Fell and Middle Knoll, but eventually the farm of Whitendale appears beyond the concave slopes, its green and velvety pastures making a fascinating contrast to the wild and remote moors that culminate in Bowland's highest hill, Ward's Stone.

The path joins a shooters' track as the ravine of Calf Clough opens out to the right. The stony track zigzags down to the valley bottom past modern

store buildings and through the farmyard.

Turn right along a stony track though gates to the west of the farmhouse. It forges north by the Whitendale River and alongside pleasant mixed woodland. Ignore the left fork, which crosses the river via a bridge: the track required on this occasion stays with the eastern banks before climbing to a grassy shelf amid high pastures.

A wooden post, the first of many on this section, marks the place where the track should be abandoned (GR657557). A footpath continues north to a five-bar gate in the wall at the top of the field. Through the gate, a worn path over rough grassland veers north-west between two small spruce plantations and across hillslopes parallel with the river.

After fording a stream, Higher Stony Clough, the well-waymarked path climbs away from the Whitendale River on hillslopes cloaked with grass, bracken and heather.

After another half-mile it meets a rutted track, the Hornby Road, under the grassy flanks of Bowland's second highest peak, White Hill.

The Hornby Road, sometimes referred to as the Salter Fell track, was constructed for most of its length along the course of an old Roman route, that linked forts at Hadrian's Wall and Ribchester. Later it was used as a packhorse route for traders whose Galloway ponies would have lugged panniers of salt from Morecambe Bay to the towns of East Lancashire.

Retrospective views down Whitendale show the river snaking through a dark moorland corridor shaded by the smooth, rounded hills of Fair Snape, Totridge and Whin Fell. The rocky knoll peeping over fellsides to the right is Wolfhole Crag and you may spy some waterfalls in a ravine beneath Esp Crag.

Turn right along the Hornby Road. Initially it is quite marshy but soon transforms into a stony cart track entering the wild basin of the Croasdale Valley. Here it descends into the wide hollow with the distant fields of the Hodder Valley contrasting with the heather-clad, stony moors.

After passing a shooters' hut and zigzagging beneath the disused quarries of Croasdale Fell, the waters of Stocks Reservoir come back into view, as does the escarpment of Pendle Hill. The track meets the outward route at the five-bar gate GR693548, and steps can be retraced to Slaidburn by way of Shay House. Alternatively take the quiet lanes, passing near to the Craft Centre at Wood House en route.

8 Beacon Fell and the Brock Valley

Beacon Fell is a little hill, easily reached by anyone with a car. On its own it's no more then a 20-minute outing, but it can be combined with the leafy little glen of the Brock to make a very pleasant and gentle route – perhaps one of the best low routes in Bowland.

Distance:
5½ miles/9km
Height gain:
575ft/175m
Walking time: 3 hours
Type of walk:
Moderately easy walk on well-maintained paths on Beacon Fell followed by narrow paths through woodland. Short stretches in the middle of the Brock Valley can be muddy after wet weather.
Start/Finish: Brock Mill car park. GR548431.
Map: OS Outdoor Leisure 41: Forest of Bowland.

After buying Beacon Fell in 1969 for recreation purposes, Lancashire County Council had much remedial work to organise, for the Sitka spruce, larch and pine were overplanted and many were diseased. In a woodland management scheme the trees were thinned out and supplemented by the planting of rowan, birch, alder and oak. Today wildlife is abundant and includes the red grouse, chaffinch, willow warbler, skylark, meadow pipit, and also foxes, stoats and rabbits.

The Brock Mill car park at the start of the walk overlooks the twisting wooded valley of the River Brock, a tributary of the Wyre. Turn right along White Lee Lane, which crosses the Brock before climbing amid farmland to a T-junction at the foot of Beacon Fell.

The signposted footpath up the hill begins at a stile, staggered to the right across the road. It crosses a field before climbing steeply through scrubland, newly planted with small trees.

Take the right fork of two narrow paths. After maintaining direction across the next field, the route enters the Beacon Fell conifer plantations at the intersection of a dry stone wall and fence. After a short distance the path comes to the narrow tarmac lane that encircles the high slopes of the fell. Across the road the path, a luxurious bed of pine needles, re-enters the conifer woods, passing the clearing of the Fell House car park and picnic site.

Turn left turn along the wide track at the far end of the site. It takes the route through more woodland to the edge of high moorland. Turn right here to climb to the summit trig point.

To the north, across the fields of Bleasdale, the shapely fells of Fair Snape and Parlick look particularly inviting. Over their shoulder, verdant pastures spread and pale to the Irish Sea.

From the summit, descend eastwards across slopes of heather and bilberry, keeping to the top edge of the conifer plantations before reaching an old quarry (now a car park).

A surfaced track continues by the north side of a large, rushy pool to a country lane. Turn left, then right at the next junction for a few strides before abandoning the lanes for a footpath on the left-hand side of the road (GR575427). Head north-eastwards beyond the wooden roadside stile to join a grassy track descending north across farmland.

On reaching a right-hand bend, take the second and less prominent path, aiming north by a fence to a small plantation of stunted pine. Here, across a stile, bear half left to the stile at the far corner of the field. Over this second stile, head north with the fence on the right at first then the left after going through a dilapidated gate. Beyond a wooden footbridge over a dyke, the path reaches a country lane opposite a stone cottage, which was once the Dog and Partridge Inn.

Turn left along the lane and then right at the next junction at Wickins Lane End. The footpath to be followed now lies a couple of hundred yards up the lane. Refreshments are available at the Bleasdale Post Office/Cafe at Higher Brock Mill, a further 100yds/m down the road, but for those with a mind to keep going, the previously mentioned path is marked by some concrete steps climbing the roadside embankment on the left. Follow the fence on the left before turning right (GR573444) along a rutted track, ending at a stile.

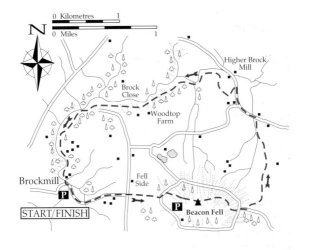

Beyond the stile the way continues, bearing left by a line of trees before entering a wooded clough by way of a stile by a five-bar gate. A well-defined path then bears right, descending through delightful mixed woodland to cross a stream on a wooden footbridge (GR568445). Turn right along a narrow path following the stream to yet another footbridge (GR565446 – don't cross) by a confluence of streams. Turn left through a narrow swathe of pastureland, with the tree-lined River Brock as a trusty companion, before re-entering the woods.

After passing close to a scout centre near Wood Top Farm, the right of way shown on the map climbs out of the glen to a metalled farm lane that descends back into the woods – probably the best route if conditions have been wet underfoot.

However, a well-used footpath continues by the riverbank, passing a newly planted oak with a plaque to the memory of prominent rambler and outdoor writer, Cyril Spiby.

The two routes meet at a footbridge across the Brock (GR553443). Keep to this side of the river, to pass a ruined cottage close to a weir, and follow a stony track for a short way. Just short of a five-bar gate, and highlighted by a tree-mounted footpath sign, a path to the right leads the way through more woodland to enter a field, which should be crossed to a stile by the riverside. From here a narrow track traces the field boundary before making an exit past some cottages to the Brock Mill car park.

Donald Dakeyne

Garstang

9 Garstang and Calder Vale

Garstang, sandwiched between the wide plains of the Fylde and the heather hills of Bowland, is the centre for many a good walk. This one wanders through woodland and over high plains before visiting a little-known vale and an even lesser known castle.

Distance: 7 miles/11km
Height gain: 590ft/180m
Walking time: 3½ hours
Type of walk: Field paths, country lanes and farm tracks
Start/Finish: Canal by Owd Tithebarne, Garstang. GR489450. Parking at large car park in the centre of Garstang.
Map: OS Outdoor Leisure 41: Forest of Bowland.

The walk begins on the towpath of the Lancaster Canal just past St Thomas's church. Walkers can gain access to it at the far side of the road bridge next to the Owd Tithebarne. The popular bar and restaurant is sited next to a large berthing area, usually full of colourful boats and hundreds of chattering people-fed ducks.

Once past the berthing area, the towpath follows the canal through fields, then heads east past a new housing estate and under the Catterall road. Now in the countryside, the iris-lined canal passes

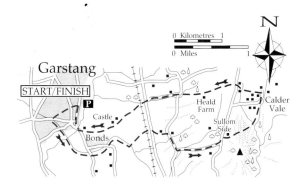

under numerous one-arched stone bridges and alongside open fields. The odd boat may come cruising past, temporarily scattering the ducks or waders, but within seconds all is returned to normality – life feels easy hereabouts.

The ruins of Greenhalgh Castle, which will be seen more closely later in the walk, poke out from the trees. Behind them, the heather and bracken-clad hills of western Bowland peep over rolling farmland.

At bridge number 56 (GR504447), leave the towpath. After climbing some steps and crossing the bridge, follow a cart track that leads north-east across fields. It crosses bridges over the London to Glasgow railway and the M6 motorway.

Veer left through the farmyard of Turner's Farm (GR510449) and follow the drive to the road. Pleasant tree-lined lanes now take the route to Sullom Side, where a rutted cart track climbs to the northern shoulder of Sullom Hill.

Looking ahead, the meadows descend to the wooded glen of Calder Vale, while the shapely Fair Snape Fell and Parlick soar above rolling farmland.

Go through the left of the two gates and follow the wire fence on the right downhill to a gate at the top edge of the woods. The path beyond, which can be a little overgrown in high summer, descends further to meet a stony track running along the valley bottom, where it passes a secluded row of terraced cottages.

The track continues through the glen above the west bank of the river. In late spring bluebells embellish the scene. Across the river, a row of cottages peeps through the trees. The route emerges from the woods just west of Calder Vale.

This little mill village is something of an enigma. Secretively sited between the wooded glen and the end of a rural cul-de-sac, its seclusion from the rest of England is both geographical and cultural. Founded and planned by the Quaker Jackson family it has no pub – the nearest, The Moorcock, is a mile away on the Oakenclough-Chipping road. The cottages are clustered around a huge stone-built mill, which is still operating today.

To continue along the route from the end of the valley track (GR532457), follow some stone steps up the grassy bank on the opposite side of the road. A narrow scrub-lined lane goes behind some houses. At its end, a waymarked path continues west across two fields, which have stiles at their boundaries. Cross the primitive footbridge to pass to the right of a whitewashed cottage (GR528457).

Soon afterwards, beyond a wooden stile on the right, a grassy track takes the route past another cottage to the roadside. Cross the road and climb a small stile, then head across fields by a fence and line of trees.

At the top of the hill the path looks down on extensive flatland fields of the Fylde, which fade to the misty blue outlines of the coast.

Descend towards Heald Farm, keeping by the fence. Watch out for a stile on the right just before the farmyard. It marks the start of a path heading west through the trees to meet a concrete farm track, which skims the southern edge of Heald Wood before reaching the road at a sharp corner.

Follow the lane westwards past Clarkson's Farm. At its terminus a track crosses the M6 and the London-Glasgow railway before joining a path heading just south of west across fields past Castles Wood. The path crosses the cutting of an old railway siding, and continues south-west across more fields towards Greenhalgh Castle Farm.

The path joins a dirt track leading past the farmhouse and the ruined castle, which was built in 1490 for the Earl of Derby. The track becomes a metalled lane and leads past a school to the Catterall road, where a right turn takes the route back to the town centre. Turn left through a ginnel by the King's Arms in Market Street to return to the car park.

10 Nicky Nook

Nicky Nook is a little hill overlooking the fields of the Fylde and overlooked by the dark moors of Bowland. It's a popular place during weekends and sunny summer afternoons but provides many interesting itineraries. This circular walk from the attractive village of Scorton takes in some of the wilder environs above the Grizedale Reservoirs, cameo landscapes of village, lake, fast-flowing stream, woodland and windswept moors.

Distance:
6 miles/10km
Height gain:
935ft/285m
Walking time: 3¹/₂ hours
Type of walk: A moderate hill climb, but most of the route is on well defined farm tracks and footpaths.
Start/Finish: Scorton village. GR502488.
Map: OS Outdoor Leisure 41: Forest of Bowland.

Climb out of Scorton's picturesque village along Snowhill Lane, which crosses the busy M6 motorway before winding by some woods to a T-junction at the foot of Nicky Nook.

The footpath opposite climbs the gorse-interspersed, grassy slopes of the hill. It passes a tiny reservoir before reaching the wilder environs of The Tarn, a desolate sheet of water, high on the hillside and fringed by some gaunt, weatherbeaten pines. The path climbs further to a concrete trig point crowning the hilltop.

Views of Bowland's heather-clad grouse moors now supplement the wide western panoramas across the forests and lakes of Wyresdale Park and the flatlands of the Fylde. Blackpool Tower and Heysham power station are clearly discernible on a coastline that includes Morecambe Bay and the pale, jagged outlines of the Lakeland Fells.

From the trig point, maintain direction to a drystone wall, which should be kept to the left when descending the bracken-clad slopes to Grizedale Reservoir.

On reaching the shores of the reservoir, turn left along a gravel track, which continues north through pleasant woodland, liberally spread with rhododendron bushes. Beyond the woodland, the track meanders through pastureland to meet a tarmac drive that takes the route eastwards to Fell End Farm.

Turn right at the farmhouse, passing through the farmyard and climbing on a stony track to the foot of a small hill. After about 100yds/m, go through a gate in the fence to the left and continue south-east on a faint path through fields, passing through a couple of five-bar gates. The path becomes more defined, and turns to the left by some woods surrounding Grizedale Brook (GR534490). It soon joins a high country lane beneath Grizedale Fell, a wild moorland spur on the western fringe of high Bowland.

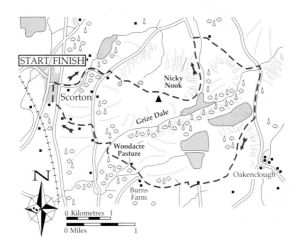

The lane leads southwards, passing the stark, wind-ruffled waters of Grizedale Lea Reservoir. Take the second track on the right, ignoring North West Water's reservoir road. After passing close to a wireless station, follow the metalled lane on the right to Moor House Farm. Beyond the farm, a grassy, enclosed track heads westwards before winding down to Burns Farm.

Go right here, taking the track at the edge of the farmyard to the terminus of a country lane, where the track zigzags to some woods, crosses Oxen Beck and heads north-west past a covered reservoir.

A stile at the end of the track marks the start of a field path, which crosses a small footbridge over a brook before a short climb to Woodacre Pasture. Bear half left at the field corner, and descend to the woods (trackless). A stile at the bottom right corner of the field allows entry into picturesque woodland of oak and beech. A steep descent follows to a footbridge over Grizedale Brook.

On crossing the footbridge, take the footpath marked 'to Higher Lane'. Turn right on reaching the lane, then left at Tithe Barn Lane, which leads back to Scorton and the excellent Priory Cafe in the village centre.

11 Fair Snape Fell

Fair Snape Fell, situated on the south-west of a horseshoe ridge of hills south of the Trough of Bowland, rises gracefully from the green fields of Bleasdale. Its sleek grassy slopes form a skyline profile not unlike a gigantic whale, with neighbour Parlick aping its tail.

Distance:
7½ miles/12km
Height gain:
1,410ft/430m
Walking time: 4 hours
Type of walk: Rough peat-hagged moorland with country lane approaches.
Start/Finish: Car park, Chipping. GR622433.

Map: OS Outdoor Leisure 41: Forest of Bowland.
Access: The section on the high ridges between Saddle Fell and Parlick is part of an access agreement and can be closed on shooting days between August 12 and December 10.

The classic route approaches Fair Snape from the south. Although cars can be parked at Fell Foot or Wolfen Mill, much closer to the hills, I have chosen to start from Chipping village, where less disruptive parking space is available.

Take the road leading north-west from the parish church, then the right fork, past Berry's Chair Works. It comes to a delightful old mill pond inhabited by some mallards. On the opposite side of the road, a stile by a drive entrance marks the start of a waymarked footpath climbing northwards over fields.

The steep-sided Parlick, Wolf Fell and Saddle Fell soon show themselves across the pastures. A post in the middle of the field highlights the place where the path divides. This route takes the left fork, descending slightly to pass some old quarries, which are now largely cloaked by grass. It then descends further to cross the tree-enshrouded Dobson's Brook on a wooden footbridge before climbing out of its little valley to a gate by Windy Hill Farm.

Turn left along a cart track that winds amid trees and rolling pastureland to a high country lane beneath the imposing spur of Saddle Fell. Here, go straight ahead on the drive to Saddle End Farm. At the north end of the farmyard, a signpost points the way along a rutted track heading north-west past a small plantation of conifers and into the Bowland Access Area.

To the left, the rough, unkempt pastures of Greenlough Clough are engulfed by the bracken and heather of Wolf Fell and Parlick. The cart track veers right to climb the spur of Saddle Fell. In the middle stages there are a number of grooved tracks to choose from. The choice isn't critical as they all meet uphill, but the correct route has a few cairns.

The twin escarpments of Longridge Fell and Pendle Hill dominate retrospective views across the attractive bowl of the Burnslack Valley. The latter lies beyond the smoky

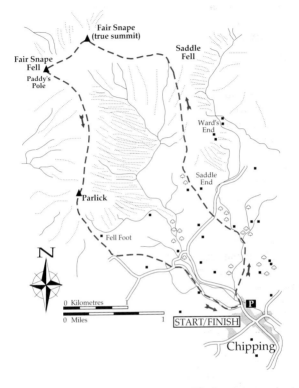

plume of the West Bradford Cement Works.

As the track approaches the main ridge it veers west onto Wolf Fell, offering an easy route through rough, peat-hagged terrain that lies across the stile in a fence at GR607473. Beyond it the shooters' track fades into the mosses and peat of the moor, finally giving up near the ridge fence just short of Fair Snape's highest point, the east summit

(1,707ft/521m). The modest top, marked by a pile of stones amid a morass of sticky peat, sphagnum moss and heather, lies close to an intersection of fences.

To reach the more popular west summit, follow the fence leading south-west until it veers left. Here, head west-south-west across rough, peat-hagged terrain – a few shallow and gravelly channels make the going easier in places.

The second summit is 1,675ft/510m high, lies on firm ground at the fell's western edge, and yields superb far-reaching views over the Fylde plains to Blackpool Tower and further northwards to the Lakeland peaks, which lie across Morecambe Bay. It has all the furniture associated with true summits – a large stone shelter, trig point and a huge cairn with resident pole (Paddy's Pole).

On the return journey the route transforms into a delightful ridge walk towards the southern outlier, Parlick. A cairned track traces the western edge of the fell before plummeting to Nick's Chair, which is said to be a favoured spot of the Devil himself.

At the col the path changes to the opposite side of the ridge fence at a ladder stile. The route now climbs the grassy slopes to Parlick's summit, where a magnificent panorama is now pasted across the horizon. In it the intricate designs formed by winding country lanes, hedgerows, scattered farmhouses and copses compose a gentle, more verdant landscape, pleasingly contrasting with the spartan moorland. This is also a popular spot for paragliders: on Parlick, you're seldom alone.

The descent from Parlick is short, steep and quick. The wide path follows the line of a deep clough swooping south-east to Fell End Farm.

South of the farm and the concrete drive to Wolfen Hall, a footpath begins at a stile on the left hand side of the lane. There are no traces on the ground, and the field boundaries shown on the map have changed with the demolition of some walls and the building of new fences elsewhere. Head eastwards across the fields, scaling a stile in a cross fence before veering half right and descending to a stile in a wall corner. A path develops, heading south-east to a roadside stile close to the right of two farmhouses. At the adjacent road junction, turn right and follow the lane back to Chipping.

12 Totridge and Bleadale Water

Totridge will be relatively unknown to law-abiding Lancashire walkers, for, until recently, this shapely hill, which figures in the standard postcard view of the Trough, has been out of bounds. It's a fine hill, well worth visiting. Other concessionary routes into the wild ravine of Bleadale Water followed by a rough ridge walk complete this itinerary for the moorland connoisseur.

Distance:
7¹/₂ miles/12km
Height gain:
1,310ft/400m
Walking time: 4¹/₂ hours
Type of walk: A tough moorland walk that requires good navigational abilities. Fording Langden Brook and Bleadale Water could be tricky after heavy rain or melting snow. Snow and ice would also make the little path above Bleadale Water treacherous.
Start/Finish: Langden Intake, Sykes. GR633512.
Map: OS Outdoor Leisure 41: Forest of Bowland.
Access: The route can be closed on shooting days between August 12 and December 10 and at times of high fire risk.

Start on the metalled water company drive through an avenue of trees, holly bushes and rhododendron. Once past the Langden Intake waterworks the tarmac ends and a stony track follows Langden Brook through a long moorland valley.

The shallow brook, which flows over a wide boulder-strewn bed, is shaded in places by oak, birch and rowan, but the trees thin out as the landscape becomes wilder.

The tree-enshrouded crags of Holdron Castle cap the hillsides on the right. Beneath them, the track divides. Take the left fork, which stays lower, eventually descending to a little stone-built shooting cabin that turns out to be Langden Castle. My belief is that the castle is a map-maker's myth and that the name probably referred to a natural rocky tor, like nearby Holdron Castle.

Beyond the castle, head south, crossing the stony brook into the side valley of Bleadale Water. The concessionary route, a faint track at first, crosses Bleadale Water beneath Sykes Fell and follows its east bank through the steep-sided clough.

Ignore the route crossing the river into Brown Berry Clough and the shooters' track to Hareden Fell at GR611493. Instead, follow the lower path by the brookside.

As the ravine narrows, the path clambers ever higher above the river and struggles to keep a hold on loose, shaly slopes. In a few places the path disappears with landslip and the walker will find him or herself grasping at the heather for a steadying handrail. Take care!

Twisted trees still decorate the austere clough, often yawning over the river to escape the deep shadows of the crags. In a side valley to the right, an unnamed stream tumbles over rocks to form an impressive waterfall.

The path has been getting fainter, and all but disappears on the heather slopes near Bleadale Grains. Be content to climb south to the ridge fence at Beasley's Steady, then turn east where some typically stodgy Bowland peat groughs await.

This is Bowland at its toughest, but maybe its wildest and best. I remember coming here several winters ago with fellow writer, Roy Clayton. Time after time, one or the other of us slipped and were up to our necks in snow.

On Fair Oak Fell the ridge fence, which has been veering left, corrects its direction with a 90° left turn. The path follows suit, heading north-east towards the summit of Totridge.

Views have been wide, with the dark heather-clad moors rising like waves to the high Ward's Stone ridge. The paler outlines of Whernside, Ingleborough and Pen-y-Ghent appear on the horizon like boats on this dark sea.

The ridge fence becomes a ridge wall on the climb to Totridge, but just short of the summit it veers right to descend into the valley. Continue north-east to the trig point.

From Totridge views are at their best east of the trig point, where the precipitous flanks tumble to the green fields of the Hodder Valley. Dunsop Bridge shelters beneath the bracken-clad Beatrix Fell, while to the east

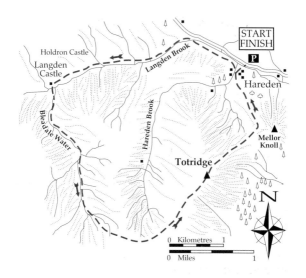

little limestone knolls and woodland interrupt a crazed pattern of drystone walls.

The new concessionary route rakes down the steep slopes towards a col at the foot of Mellor Knoll. Its official line aims for the apex of a bend in Broad Head's intake wall. The slopes of bracken, heather and bilberry are steep and friable, and many walkers have followed a more sensible line on a narrow sheeptrack along the edge of the fell to GR636491 before descending north-east down the nab of the hill to reach and follow the previously mentioned wall. The wall now guides the path to meadowland at the head of Lane Foot Beck.

There are very pleasant views down the hollow of Lane Foot Beck to the Hareden Valley, where a whitewashed farm cottage lies dwarfed by the bracken-clad hillsides of Hareden Nab and Staple Oak Fell.

The path, still following the wall, climbs from the meadows towards the bridleway at the foot of grassy Mellor Knoll. At the time of writing there is no stile or gate in the wall at the junction of the routes but I am assured that they will be in place by the time you read this.

Turn left along the bridleway, climbing over the ladder stile and descending across fields to Riggs Plantation where a cart track is encountered. Leave the cart track after just a few paces to cross another ladder stile, and descend fields on a trackless route into the Hareden Valley. It crosses Hareden Brook on a footbridge and turns right by Hareden Farm on a surfaced lane.

Heading east, the lane crosses the wider Langden Brook on a large concrete bridge, but don't cross with it. Instead turn left through a five-bar gate, recross Hareden Brook on a stone footbridge (GR643506), then turn right by a wall to a stile by the banks of the Langden Brook. The path follows the watercourse round the perimeter of the field to cross a stile into open country. Here a well-defined grassy track heads north-west, parallel to the river.

A tatty steel footbridge allows the crossing of Langden Brook at GR632511 near the Langden Intake waterworks. Beyond the bridge the path goes though a strip plantation of larches, then, beyond a step-stile, turns right on the waterworks' drive back to the car park on to the Trough road.

13 Stocks Reservoir

Looking at the map you could be forgiven for thinking that this walk would be dominated by sprucewoods, but you would be wrong. Where the walk does enter the forest, it keeps to the edge, where the trees are a pleasing mix of broadleaved and conifer. Stocks Reservoir fits well into the scene, surrounded by pasture in a shallow bowl overlooked by dusky moors. This classic walk from Slaidburn rounds the lake, before taking a look at the Croasdale valley, which lies in the shadow of the Bowland fells.

Distance: 9½ miles/16km
Height gain: 885ft/270m
Walking time: 5-6 hours
Type of walk: Fairly leisurely walk on good field paths and tracks
Start/Finish: Car park, Slaidburn. GR714524.
Map: OS Outdoor Leisure 41: Forest of Bowland.

From the car park walk back through the village turning right along the lane by the war memorial. At the far side of the bridge over Croasdale Brook go through a kissing gate on the right, and head north-east across the fields to an external wall corner. From here the path keeps the wall to the left and joins a track that crosses the River Hodder at Holmhead Bridge.

Beyond the bridge the track climbs roughly parallel to the tree-lined river to reach Hammerton Hall.

This stately 16th-century mansion was home to the Hammerton family until 1536, when they were involved in the Pilgrimage of Grace, a Northern English protest against the destruction of minor monasteries. For his part Sir Stephen Hammerton was hanged, drawn and quartered and the lands, including Hammerton Hall, were confiscated.

The track circumvents the hall, turning right, (north-east) beyond it. Take the left gate shortly after, climbing north-north-east by a wall towards a spruce plantation bordering the Stocks Reservoir dam. The green track traces the east edge of the plantations before turning sharp right on Ten Acre Hill where it descends to Black House Farm. Keep the farm to the right, then follow its stony access road over Rushton Hill.

By now the Stocks Reservoir has come into full view. Surrounding green fields and woodland are topped by the dark hillsides of Dunsop Fell and the crinkled craggy skyline of Bowland Knotts. This part of the Hodder Valley was dammed and flooded in 1925 to supply Blackpool. Stocks in Bolland, a village comprising a church, 20 or so houses, a shop, a smithy and pub called the Travellers Rest, was lost forever. It was sited between the island and the near shoreline.

The stony track meets the road by St James's Church and the south-west extremity of the Gisburn Forest. Stones used in the church's construction were taken from the old church,

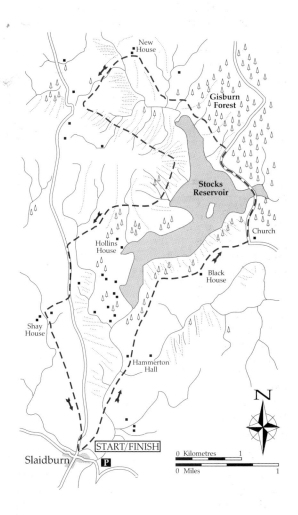

New House

Gisburn Forest

Stocks Reservoir

Church

Hollins House

Black House

Shay House

Hammerton Hall

START/FINISH

P

Slaidburn

N

0 Kilometres 1

0 Miles 1

which was dismantled to make way for the reservoir.

Turn left past the church following the road, whose verges are filled with red campion, meadowsweet, and hemlock, through the conifers of the Gisburn Forest. Leave the road for the car park on the bend at GR733564.

A track from the back of the car park continues north-west through pleasant woodland. Ignore the left fork, which leads to a lakeside hide and the right fork, a formal forest walk. Instead maintain direction to a ruined stone building, where the path veers left to a stile and gate at the edge of the plantation.

In the view ahead, the infant Hodder meanders through lush green fields. On the skyline its valley is tighter, confined by the stark stony slopes of Catlow Fell.

The path traverses fields, descending westwards to cross Hasgill Beck on a stone-built one-arched bridge. The pleasant beck, shaded by sycamores, flows playfully across a stony bed and was full of small trout, when I last visited.

From the bridge, the path climbs north-west across more pastureland to the ruins of New House, which must have been an impressive hillside hamlet before its demise. Turn left by a stile and gate on a clear path that zigzags down to some stepping stones across the Hodder.

On the other side, the path climbs to the ruins of

Collyholme at the foot of Copped Hill Clough. The path turns left through the old farmyard, crossing the stream, which hereabouts is covered by gritstone slabs. After passing left of an old stone water trough climb south-west on a path parallel to the tree enshrouded clough.

The way is never in doubt as there are stiles in the field borders. As the Slaidburn to Bentham road appears, the path meets a good track. Turn left along it and go through the first gate, but leave it here for a less well-defined green track that begins on the right, across an area of rushes.

The track, which soon establishes itself, is the course of a narrow gauge railway that was built to supply stone for the construction of the Stocks Reservoir dam. The depressions where the old sleepers would have been are still clearly visible. Beyond Copter Syke, the old track goes through a cutting. Marker posts highlight the route as it curves to the right.

Stocks Reservoir has come into view again. This time the backcloth includes Pendle Hill, peeping out behind the more sombre slopes of Waddington Fell.

The track should be abandoned north of Hollins House. A footpath signpost points the way along a faint waymarked path climbing west past another ruin, then round the top edge of some woodland. Beyond the woodland it descends to a firm cart track that leads to the Slaidburn road at GR709553.

Turn left along the narrow hedge-lined country

lane then right on a farm lane, which descends into Croasdale towards Shay House farm.

A footpath begins from a stile on the left, near the bridge over Croasdale Brook. The path heads south, following the brook at first, but maintaining direction to a stile in the far end of the field where the brook bends right. Keep to the right in the next field to locate the stile in its bottom corner.

The brook has come back to the path here but the path shuns it, veering slightly left to climb by some hawthorn trees to the top of a hill. Keep to the same south-south-east direction, using the stiles in cross-walls and fences. As the Slaidburn road draws closer, a drystone wall on the left forces the path to follow it and go south. It meets the road beyond a stile just short of the bridge over Croasdale Brook, which was encountered earlier in the day. Follow the lane through Slaidburn village back to the car park.

Thirsty walkers may note that for the Hark to Bounty pub turn right at the war memorial.

14 Downham and Sawley

Of all the routes in the book, this one has the most attractive scenery. True, it's not the wildest or most dramatic, but Constable would have loved it. Round every corner, there's something to see: everything's so green and fresh. Go on a fine spring day and leave some time for a riverside picnic.

> **Distance:** 6 miles/10km
> **Height gain:** 490ft/150m
> **Walking time:** 3-4 hours
> **Type of walk:** An easy walk across fields and by the riverside with only one climb – on the shoulder of Worsaw Hill.
> **Start/Finish:** Car park/information centre, Downham. GR785442.
> **Map:** OS Landranger 103: Blackburn and Burnley or Outdoor Leisure 41: Forest of Bowland.

Downham shelters under Pendle Hill and its attendant limestone knoll, Worsaw Hill. It's a pleasing village with a green, a stream running through, a good pub and a square-towered church that looks down over the rooftops.

Walk up the street from the car park towards the church before turning right just past the Assheton Arms. Beyond a gate into a field, the path required climbs northwards by some woodland.

A marker post showing a white waymarking arrow shows the direction of a Roman road, but on this occasion, ignore it and continue to the northern brow of the hill. From here the required path, initially non-existent on the ground, veers north-east, aiming for a limestone crag capped with tall trees. A lone hawthorn bush highlights the path raking down the steepest bit of the descent.

On reaching the previously mentioned crag, the path veers left to a step-stile in a fence, where a left turn follows to the Rimington Lane at GR787451. Across the lane the continuing path traces the south-western edge of Newfield Woods and under the railway bridge. To the right a 12-arched railway viaduct spans the pretty little wooded glen of Ings Beck. The path descends by some larch trees and to the right to cross the lively beck on a fine stone packhorse bridge. This is one of the many fine picnic spots on the walk.

Beyond the bridge, the path climbs half left up a grassy bank to a stile, then traverses fields in a north-west direction, crossing several stiles en route to the A59. On the other side of the road, the route maintains direction across a small meadow and over a stile to a track enclosed by trees and a hedge. This ends at a metalled farm lane.

The new path begins across the lane and heads north-west with the wide Ribble Valley unfolding across the fields, and the houses of Sawley and Grindleton leading the eye to the bare moorland tops of Easington and Waddington Fells. As it descends, the path reveals more of Sawley Abbey.

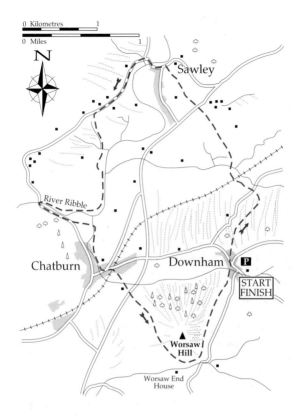

The abbey was founded by William, the third Baron
Percy, and established in 1147. Unfortunately, the
Cistercian monks lived here in poverty, and offered little
to the community. The building was destroyed during
the Dissolution and, for his courageous part in the
Pilgrimage of Grace the last Abbot, William Trafford, was
put to death.

After passing the abbey, the path terminates in the car park of the Spread Eagle pub. Take the Grindleton road to the splendid three-arched Sawley Bridge spanning the Ribble, then follow the riverside path, which cuts a corner before returning to the road. Pendle Hill can now be seen reflecting in the rippling waters of the Ribble.

The tarmac doesn't last long. After climbing past the Bowland High School to a bend in the road, a signposted footpath to the left now heads south across fields to reacquaint itself with the river. It crosses two stiles and a little footbridge along the way.

The path follows the grassy flood embankments close to the river, except for one short section where the eroded banks have necessitated a minor diversion on the other side of a fence. The path meets the road at the bridge by Riverside Mill. Turn left to cross the bridge and follow the road by the river to the first bend. Here a cart track on the left heads east but the right of way leaves it almost immediately for the Ribble's south bank.

Across a footbridge the path turns right to pass a sewage works. The path soon leaves the eyesore behind as a hedge on the left guides the route uphill across fields with Chatburn's spired church on the skyline ahead. After entering the local sports field, the path passes to the right of the church and onward to Sawley Road.

Cross the road, then take the road half left by the Chatburn Tyre Depot. Beyond the bridge over the railway, turn right along Robinson Street to a T-junction. Now follow the unsurfaced Kayley Lane, signposted as a footpath to Worston. The lane twists past some cottages and terraced housing. A waymark shows the spot where the footpath turns right. After a short way, turn left through a gap stile in a wall. The path now turns right and follows the perimeter of a lawned area to reach the A59 to the right of a house. Again, cross this busy road with care.

On the other side stands Worsaw Hill, a splendid limestone knoll. The route tackles its north-west slopes after crossing fields. Although many walkers have aimed for the summit, the right of way, once on the shoulder of the hill, heads south.

In fact the right of way is the superior route, and soon follows a lovely green track beneath grassy slopes studded with crags and hawthorn trees. It all feels like the Yorkshire Dales at their best. Ahead lies Pendle Hill, its more sombre slopes scattered with the darker hues of gritstone.

The grassy track veers left to skirt the southern end of the hill, drawing close to Worsaw End Farm. Do not be lured onto farm tacks here, but turn north-east through a squeeze stile into fields east of the hill. A fence/hedge on the left guides the route back towards Downham, whose houses appear beyond Longlands Wood. Keep the woods to the left as the path declines gradually into the village, where it threads between some cottages to emerge to the right of the car park entrance.

15 Clitheroe Castle and Whalley Abbey

In the heart of the Ribble Valley lies Clitheroe, its austere Norman castle staring across to Pendle Hill and down river to Whalley. This route samples the magic and the turbulent history of the area, initially choosing to climb to the lower hillslopes, synonymous with witches, before going down to the riverside. On the way it takes in Clitheroe's castle and the abbey and tea shops of Whalley.

Distance: *12½ miles/20km*	***Start/Finish:*** *Spring Wood Car Park & Picnic Site, Whalley. GR741361.*
Height gain: *790ft/240m*	
Walking time: *6 hours*	***Map:*** *OS Landranger 103: Blackburn and Burnley or Outdoor Leisure 41: Forest of Bowland with OS Explorer 19: West Pennine Moors.*
Type of walk: *A long but moderately easy circular walk starting with a climb over moorland, thence across pastureland on field, riverside paths and lanes.*	

The signposted footpath begins from the roadside 20yds/m south of the car park and climbs fields between the golf course and Spring Wood. Cross the footbridge at the top end of the wood and follow the faint path that heads north-east to a stile at the top corner of the field. Beyond another stile a few yards further, the path turns right, tracing the northern boundary walls of the large Clerk Hill house, where a drive climbs eastwards to a metalled lane (GR 749364).

Turn left along the lane, which degenerates into a track beyond Wiswell Moor Farm. This continues north-east at the edge of rough moorland high above the Sabden valley, scene of many of the sinister tales of the Pendle witches.

Two families, led by their elder women, Elizabeth Southern (Old Demdike) from Newchurch and Anne Whittle (Chattox) from near Pendle Hall were involved in many of these tales.

In 1612 Alizon Device, a granddaughter of Chattox, put a curse on a peddler after he refused to buy some pins. The peddler suffered a stroke and fell to the ground. Alizon admitted her sins to the local magistrate and turned in the Demdike and Chattox clans. The witches, 19 in all, were sent for trial at Lancaster and subsequently put to death.

The track emerges at the crest of the high road near the Nick of Pendle. Turn left along the road past the Wells Springs pub and the Pendle dry ski run before turning off on a narrow footpath on the right that descends north across rough moorland. It crosses a brook on a small footbridge close to the stone-built Howcroft Barn, which lies in the shadow of Pendle Hill's sullen northern slopes.

The route continues to the right of another barn and descends along a groove in high pastures

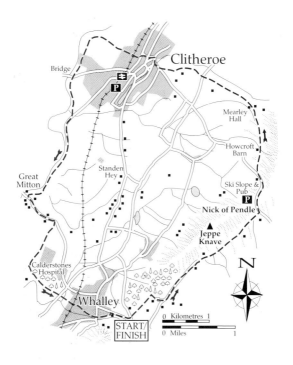

through a red gate and on to a farm lane. Turn right along the lane, then left shortly afterwards on a track that passes to the right of Mearley Hall. It continues over fields to cross the busy A59.

A signposted footpath on the other side of the road leads across a narrow metalled lane (the course of the old A59) and traverses more fields. It keeps to the left of a hedge of holly, hawthorn and wild roses to reach a farm road that leads to the outskirts of Clitheroe. Frequent tourist signs point the way through the pleasant little town to the castle, which perches on a gigantic limestone crag at its heart.

Clitheroe Castle's origins are uncertain but it is thought to have been constructed around the 12th century for the powerful Norman family, the De Laceys.

From the north of the castle, follow signs to the railway station, beyond which turn left under the railway bridge on a winding street that passes a car park and the modern housing of Black Lane Croft. Turn right along Kirkmoor Road, then follow a footpath traversing fields towards the River Ribble. The building on the far banks is Waddow Hall.

Turn left on a gravel path parallel to the banks of the River Ribble. Beyond a gate the route joins a farm lane to the village of Low Moor. Maintain direction on the street between the houses and follow the Ribble Way signs across some playing fields. Another Ribble Way signpost points the way left between the Ribblesdale swimming pool and the squash courts to the B-road. A right turn along the road leads to Edisford Bridge, site of a fierce battle between the Normans and Scots.

From the bridge, follow the riverside path past the camping and caravan site. Turn left along an enclosed path, then left along Henthorne Road to Fishes and Peggy Hill. Here take the track past Shuttleworth Farm, continuing along field paths by the Ribble to emerge by the Aspinall Arms at Great Mitton, where they do very appetising bar meals.

After turning left along the B-road past the Mitton Hall hotel, leave the road for a stony track on the right, tracing the perimeters of Calderstones Hospital. Abandon the track at its southern extremity (GR722367) for a path that heads south-east beyond a small gate, tracing the banks of a streamlet across fields. It passes beneath the road bridge carrying the A59 over the wide, meandering River Calder to join a track that continues under the expansive, 49-arch, brick railway viaduct. Stay with the track into Whalley where it passes through an impressive stone gateway and the ancient ruins of Whalley Abbey.

Abbot Gregory of Norbury and about 20 monks set up the Cistercian Abbey at the turn of the 13th century. Like many other beautiful abbeys, it was destroyed following the Reformation. Its ruins are now open to the public along with a cafe and the Memory Lane Museum, which are also within the grounds. The nearby church is well known for its pre-conquest crosses and is believed to have been built on the site of a church dating back to AD600.

On leaving the abbey, continue along the lane to the main street with its Tudor and Georgian buildings, then turn right towards the river. Just before the bridge, follow a ginnel on the left, marked with a public footpath sign. It passes some charming cottages on its way to the river banks by a large weir. Trace the river banks for a short while, until the path diverts left climbing past a farm to the B6246 road. This leads back to Spring Wood Car Park.

16 Pendle H
Sabden

Below, the Ch...
plantatio...
peace...
sq...

One of the more unusual routes to P...
the hillside above Sabden, first ... ...e wild
Deerstones, Pendle's rockiest place. It's a fine walk for an
autumn day when the broadleaved woodland seen early
in the route would complement the wide panoramas seen
from Scout Cairn and the summit.

Distance: *8 miles/13km*	***Start/Finish:*** *Lower car*
Height gain:	*park south of the Nick of*
1,080ft/330m	*Pendle. GR773384*
Walking time: *5 hours*	***Map:*** *OS Landranger*
Type of walk: *A*	*103: Blackburn and*
moderate walk starting	*Burnley or Outdoor*
quite high, but crossing	*Leisure 41: Forest of*
high exposed moorland	*Bowland.*

Follow the track from the car park eastwards
between the moorland slopes and high pastures
above Sabden. Near Calf Hill, the sunken track
crosses Badger Well Water (GR779386) and climbs
north-east away from the pastures to the lower hill
slopes.

The track degenerates into a narrow footpath that
fords an unnamed clough to enter an attractive
area dotted with oak and rowan.

urn Clough Reservoir shelters beneath a of conifers. Looking south, Sabden looks , tucked in its pastoral valley and shaded by a at, pastured ridge flecked with woodland.

The path continues as a worn, peaty channel running alongside a crumbling wall at the top edge of the conifer woods. Where the woodland perimeter turns north, the path follows suit. Beyond the woods it continues north, climbing through thick bracken. The clough on the left acts as a guide, as do the Deerstones rocks on the horizon.

The bracken relents above the 375m contour and the path swings right on a grassy spur to the top of the Deerstones, a wild place that is strewn with boulders.

The path degenerates beyond Deerstones. Turn north across the grassy top to the ridge wall and follow it east to the ladder stile. Beyond the stile, head north-west across Spence Moor, with the depression of Ogden Clough to the right. The route joins the popular path from the Nick of Pendle, heading north on rough, grassy slopes.

Turn left along the line of a collapsed wall (GR788405) following a faint path that swings right on nearing a wall corner at Pendle's northern edge. It climbs north-east across Turn Head, rounds the chasm of Mearley Clough, and continues to Scout Cairn, a huge pile of stones with a plaque commemorating 75 years of scouting.

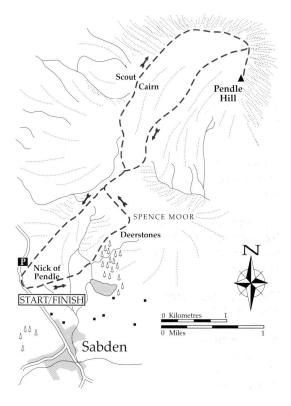

The view north from the cairn includes Clitheroe, nestling among the fields of the Ribble valley. Rising above the fields the escarpment of Longridge Fell is backed up by the higher hills of Bowland. To the west, beyond Preston and the Fylde, Blackpool Tower should be discernible, jutting out into the Irish Sea coastline and framed by the Lakeland peaks. To the east across Ribblesdale are the instantly recognisable outlines of

A clear track continues across the grasslands near the edge. It swings right to a ladder stile in a tall stone wall on Pendle's Big End. Across the stile, the way southwards leads to the summit trig point. Here the scarred eastern face of the hill plummets to the valley and rolling, verdant countryside, where Barley hides by two little knolls and two small reservoirs.

Retrace the route to the ladder stile. Do not cross this time, but turn left to follow a path into Ogden Clough. It traces the upper rim of the deepening ravine before straddling open fellsides of Black Hill. Here it continues the descent on a rutted grassy track which traverses Pendleton Moor to the Nick of Pendle's upper car park, where it's just a short walk to the lower park.

17 Black Moss and Brown Hill

Nine out of ten walkers from Barley turn their attentions to Pendle Hill, which overshadows the charming little village. But to the east, small hills, green pastures and pleasant woodland await those looking for something a little different, and, maybe, a little easier.

Distance:
4¹/₂ miles/7km
Height gain:
885ft/270m
Walking time: 2¹/₂ -3 hours
Type of walk: Fairly easy walk on unsurfaced lanes, field and woodland paths.
Start/Finish: Barley car park and information centre. GR823403.
Map: OS Landranger 103: Blackburn and Burnley or Outdoor Leisure 41: Forest of Bowland.

A Pendle Way sign (a witch on a broomstick) from the east side of the car park highlights an unsurfaced lane that follows a chattering stream to the hamlet of Narrowgates.

The stone cottages were built in the 19th-century for mill workers. The cotton mill has itself been converted into a house after ceasing production in 1967, while the old mill pool has been filled in to make way for a car park.

Through Narrowgates, the track, shaded by the

hillslopes and pine trees of Stang Top Moor, continues eastwards by the stream to White Hough, another secluded hamlet.

Whitehough Grange Farm was built in 1593 and would have been used over the centuries for both farming and weaving.

At a crossroads of routes, turn left on a metalled lane that winds above the hamlet. The next path, which lies just beyond a brick shed on the right-hand side of the lane, heads east through attractive woodland, passing the Whitehough Camp School, an outdoor centre for Lancashire children.

Leave the woods by a step-stile and turn half-left along the perimeter towards the farmhouse at Offa Hill. Ignore the first stile on the left but take the second, by the farmhouse.

A Pendle Way sign then points to the right, but the route wanted here climbs northwards keeping a fence to the right to emerge on the roadside at GR836408.

The start of the next footpath should be immediately across the road, but it has been fenced off and walkers are expected to join it on Brown Hill Farm's access track a short way north. This heads north-east on the pastured slopes of Brown Hill. Retrospective views include Pendle Hill peeping over Stang Top Moor and glimpses of the Ogden Valley.

Where the track turns left for Brown Hill Farm,

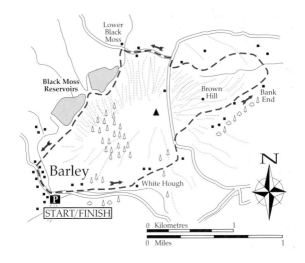

leave it and continue east on a rutted track across fields, keeping below Brown Hill's northern flanks. Beyond the next stile in a cross-wall, the path aims for a stone-built barn. After crossing a step stile in a nearby cross-wall, veer left alongside the next wall for a few yards, passing two adjacent gates before crossing another stile. Beyond this a faint path descends to the left of the barn along the pastured spur with mixed woodland to the right.

The land beneath your feet is green and pleasant – rolling, velvet hills, soft wooded valleys. Topping all this, brown moors rise to Weets Hill, where a white-painted trig point gleams on the skyline.

Soon the substantial Bank End farm appears on the right, and the path threads through sparse but newly-planted spruce trees. Take the left of two faint paths descending along the spur to a gap-stile in a brick wall, now just above the farm. The path goes through more spruce trees before turning left (north) at the next wall, crossing a stile in a fence and descending on a cart track (not marked on current maps) towards a bridge across a stream. On the nearside of the bridge, turn right across another stile to follow a short muddy path to a wooden footbridge (GR846417), which should be crossed before climbing out of the little valley, keeping a line of trees to the left.

Shortly, a cottage comes into view. As it does, the trees on the left come to an end. Turn left here and cross the stile into the next field. The path, now waymarked, heads generally westwards across a number of fields crossing several stiles and a footbridge spanning a stream.

Donald Dakeyne

Barley

Brown Hill Farm is particularly dominant, high on the hillside to the left. Immediately north of it at GR839416, climb north-west across fields to the cottage at Higher Briercliffe.

At the top of the field a waymarking arrow reassures the walker of the route, which crosses the cottage's highly decorative garden laid out across the path.

Just beyond the house, follow the metalled drive to a stile on the right marking the start of a path climbing north-west across a field to a nearby road junction. Follow the road westwards past Black Moss Farm, before turning left on North West Water's cinder track past the Upper Black Moss Reservoir.

Pendle Hill towers above the reservoir shores. On a sunless day when the waters are black and perhaps ruffled by the wind, the dark and barren slopes of Pendle's Big End exude menace and conjure up images of witchcraft and treachery.

The track divides beyond the dam of the upper reservoir. Turn left to follow the one that traces the eastern shores of Lower Black Moss Reservoir. It descends to the roadside cottages at the north end of Barley village.

18 Around the Ribble and Hodder

The Ribble and Hodder meet amid some of Lancashire's most pleasant landscapes. Hereabouts, their calm waters slowly weave through rolling pastureland, green enough and lush enough to look like golf fairways, and the rooftops and turrets of mansions rise out of woodland, looking down on little Hurst Green village like exalted castles. This leisurely walk takes in all this: the greenness and peacefulness are always prevalent.

Distance: 6 miles/10km
Height gain: 360ft/110m
Walking time: 3 hours
Type of walk: Leisurely on riverside and field paths and farm lanes
Start/Finish: Hurst Green. Roadside parking near village hall, GR684380, or on the lay-by on Whalley Road, east of the village
Map: OS Explorer 19: West Pennine Moors or Landranger 103: Blackburn and Burnley.

Follow the Stoneyhurst road south through the village to the Shireburn Arms. The path down to the River Ribble begins at a stile at the back of the pub car park and descends pastures with a hedge to the right. A Ribble Way sign ushers the route across a dyke dividing two fields. The route then reverts to its south-easterly direction, following the line of a deepening tree-lined hollow on the left.

After rounding a grassy knoll, the path goes over a stile in a fence, then across a footbridge spanning a feeder stream and into a field, where it descends to the top of some woods overlooking the River Ribble. Another stile allows the route into the woods, where steps descend to another footbridge over a stream.

Below, the wide River Ribble flows lazily, meandering through the fields. The wooded escarpment of Longridge Fell rises across the fields, aping its more distant neighbour Pendle Hill, which soars higher, but paler, into the sky.

The path goes down to join the Ribble, staying on the nearside of a wire fence to pass an aqueduct. It joins a rutted track on the approach to the cottage at Jumbles. After following the track beyond the cottage, the route temporarily eases away from the river, following a raised grassy embankment towards an abandoned house (GR707372), which was once occupied by a ferry man.

Until its closure in 1954, the ferry operated between here and Hacking Hall, an impressive 17th-century building clearly in view across the river. One of the old boats has been restored and can be seen in Clitheroe Castle's museum.

By the side of the hall the River Calder begins its course from the Ribble. So rural now, its clear waters will soon be entrapped and polluted by the factories of Padiham and Burnley.

The Ribble turns north, and the path turns with it

for a while. But the Ribble deserts our route, sneaking off through fields to the right, leaving us with another river, the Hodder. Luckily the Hodder is a fine river, a river that flows free of towns and cities.

By the confluence, the route joins an enclosed track to Winckley Hall Farm. It turns left into the farmyard, then right in front of the house, before turning left again to climb through the woodlands surrounding the impressive gothic mansion of Winckley Hall.

After rounding the hall to the north side, a stile on the right gives access to a path that heads north-west to a kissing gate. What happens in reality here is not what the map or the Ribble Way signpost suggests. The map shows a more southerly course by a small stand of trees, while the Ribble Way sign points across the field, which is usually ploughed and cropped. The farmer asks that the walker takes a short diversion to the right along the field edge, thence along the top edge of Spring Wood. The farmer's route is an easier and better course. All routes converge on the east edge of the wood.

After descending past a wet, cow-pocked area near a pond, the path descends to the road junction at GR701389. Turn right along the road, descending to Lower Hodder Bridge.

A fascinating bridge, built for Sir Richard Shireburn in 1562 and restored in 1970, spans the river next to the road bridge. The old bridge is said to have been crossed by Oliver Cromwell.

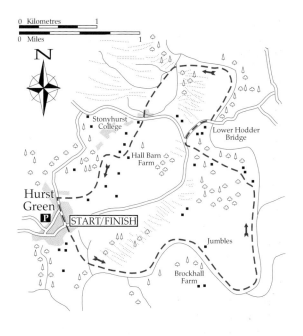

A path from the road bridge continues north-east along the west bank of the Hodder. It is one of the most beautiful parts of the walk. The river winds between flower-filled pastures and steep wooded slopes, while a gothic manor, Hodder Place, crowns a wooded hill to the north. The river and the path swing left towards the manor. On the final approaches, the route follows a wide track, climbing high above the riverbank to its northern side.

Where the track doubles back into the grounds of the manor, a narrower path takes the route west, descending to a stream crossing. Beyond this, turn left (south) following the course of the stream through attractive woodland carpeted with bluebells and wild garlic. Across a wooden footbridge, some steps climb to the top edge of the woodland, where the path makes a right turn.

After a short way, a stile allows entry into adjacent fields. Follow the hedge on the right before turning left on an unsurfaced lane that leads past some cottages to the road. Here, Stonyhurst Post Office offers refreshments.

Across the road, follow a metalled lane past St Mary's Hall. Go through the grassy ginnel to the right of Hall Barn Farm, before turning right on another metalled lane past the college cricket pitch.

Where the track bends right beyond the pitch, turn left through a gate and pass through a narrow field, keeping close to the woods on the right. The path comes to a kissing gate by a cottage aptly named Dead End. Here a street leads to the road linking Hurst Green with the main entrance to Stonyhurst College.

To see the college buildings at their most impressive, detour right to look down that straight road. Otherwise turn left back to the village.

The gatehouse of Stonyhurst formed part of the original building constructed for Sir Richard Shireburn in 1592. The building was enlarged and the last of the Shireburn line, Sir Nicholas, added the two prominent eagle-crowned cupolas and ornamental lakes.

Stonyhurst College has its origins in France, dating back to the troubled times of the Reformation. Wealthy Roman Catholics would entrust their children's education to the original school across the channel, but during the French Revolution they were forced back to England, where the Weld family donated Stonyhurst.

The college is open to the public in July and August (not Mondays) and it is well worth visiting for its splendid architecture, beautiful grounds, the museum and library.

Lancashire's South and West Pennines

Many of the South Pennines' greatest treasures lie in Calderdale and Greater Manchester, outside the Lancashire borders. The Red Rose county, however, still claims the highest summit, Lad Law on Boulsworth Hill (1,695ft/517m), and many of the places loved so dearly by the Brontë sisters.

Boulsworth Hill is largely untainted, but the meagre access has been hard won. The concessionary routes on the North West Water side of the hill allow a fine walk from the charming chocolate box village of Wycoller.

Black Hameldon has long been a favourite of mine. It's one of those places that cheer for no apparent reason. Perhaps it's those rocky outcrops that jut out like dark castles from the tops of the windswept moors with all the drama and austerity of a scene from an Emily Brontë novel. Climb a South Pennine hill and it may be yours for the day.

Ringed by the north-west towns of Blackburn, Haslingden, Bolton and Chorley, the West Pennine Moors cover 90 square miles. Perceived as the poor relations in Lancashire's family of hills, the West Pennine Moors have been criss-crossed by lines of pylons; they have been mined, quarried, and, more recently, they have been afforested with spruce.

But the West Pennines are not neglected by

walkers, who come for the intimate views of their homes in the nearby towns, and to pick out the famous buildings and landmarks on the Manchester skyline, or maybe they like to gaze across the plains of the Fylde to the golden streak that is the Lancashire coast glinting in fading sunlight.

Donald Dakeyne

Belmont

19 Darwen Hill

Darwen Hill, the northernmost West Pennine Moor, stands sentry over both Blackburn and Darwen. Although only 1,220ft/372m above sea level, its splendid position offers fine views ranging across the county to Morecambe Bay and the Lake District. This circular walk combines the hill with the lovely woodlands surrounding the Roddlesworth Reservoirs.

Distance:
5 miles/8km
Height gain:
1,110ft/340m
Walking time: 2¹/₂ hours
Type of walk: Good moorland paths and tracks combined with farm lanes and courtesy paths in the Roddlesworth area.
Start/Finish:
Sunnyhurst Woods Car Park, Darwen.
GR679225
Map: OS Explorer 19: West Pennine Moors.

From the car park, walk back down the lane to the Sunnyhurst Inn, where a tree-lined, stony cart track on the right climbs steadily westwards to the slopes of Darwen Hill. The hillsides ahead are woven with heather, sedge and bilberry, with the Jubilee Tower standing like a rocket on the skyline.

After passing overgrown quarry workings, stay with the southbound track, which climbs the hillslopes before veering south-west, and making a bee-line for the tower.

Darwen's Jubilee Tower is nearly 90 feet high. It was built in 1897 to commemorate Queen Victoria's Diamond Jubilee and the winning of free access to the moors. It was restored in 1972 after falling into disrepair.

That walkers are free to roam on Darwen Moor is largely due to the efforts of Mr W T Ashton. In 1878 he engaged in a long, hard, legal battle with the moor's owners, who had blocked rights of way and kept the moors exclusively for their shooting interests. On his death in 1894, Mr. Ashton's sons bought the shooting rights and vested them in the Corporation, thus opening the moors for all to enjoy.

Many walkers will want to climb the tower's spiral staircase to the lofty viewing platform. On clear days they will be rewarded by far-reaching panoramas. Beyond Blackburn, Darwen and the green fields of the Vale of Chipping, the hills of Bowland and the Lakeland mountains frame the pale blue seas of Morecambe Bay. Pendle Hill lies to the north-east, with the distinctive peaks of Ingleborough and Pen-y-Ghent behind it on the horizon.

Beyond the tower the route continues along Darwen Hill's north-west edge above Sunnyhurst Hey Reservoir. On the western side of the hill the wide path is joined by a fence to the right. Ignore paths descending into a wooded hollow on the right, but instead follow the one that veers gradually left (south-east) across the heathery plateau of Darwen Moor.

At a junction of routes (GR677206) take the path to the right, which crosses the fence via a stile, then descends towards Stepback Brook (not named on Landranger Maps). This, in turn, should be abandoned just before the stream crossing for a rutted track that swings right before following the eastern banks into a sylvan hollow with a small waterfall.

Beyond the falls, the path meets a fenced farm lane leading north-west beneath the woods, then across fields. After passing some terraced cottages the lane reaches the Tockholes Road, just south of the Royal Arms.

The beautiful wooded valley of Roddlesworth lies ahead. Far more paths exist in this popular local beauty spot than are shown on the OS Maps and this can be confusing. In spring the place is ablaze with the colour of an extensive bluebell carpet.

Opposite the pub, a narrow path descends west veering north-west into the woodlands. After crossing a stony track, it continues to the southern shores of the Roddlesworth Reservoir. Here the route doubles back (left) on a prominent track by the eastern banks of the River Roddlesworth before crossing on a concrete bridge. Turn right beyond the bridge along a path that can be muddy in places. It heads towards the reservoir's western shores which it then traces, keeping to the left of a stone wall.

After crossing a small stream by way of a primitive footbridge, the path exits on a Water Authority road by the large earth-fill dam. A signposted grassy footpath then crosses beneath the dam to its

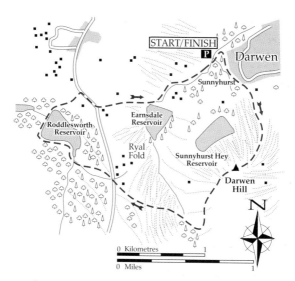

northern extremity. Turn right here for a few yards before following a path climbing to the top edge of the woods to reach a stile (GR659223). A vehicle track then crosses two fields back to the Tockholes Road. (Note: The path across the fields is a short way north of the one shown on current maps, but avoids the farmhouse.)

Follow the road to the right for a couple of hundred yds/m, leaving it for a walled farm lane that climbs east across farmland, before descending to the Earnsdale Reservoir. The pleasant lake lies in the shade beneath the Jubilee Tower and Darwen Hill's heathered northern flanks.

The route enters Sunnyhurst Woods on a stony path starting from the western side of the dam.

The attractive parkland boasts more than 250 species of flowering plants, including golden saxifrage, and is a delight to walk in all seasons. Take the lower path at the first junction, keeping to the north of the stream.

The stream should eventually be crossed on a stone bridge preceding the park's circular bandstand. A path to the right climbs south-east back to the park gates and the car park. Maybe it's time for some tea and cakes at the Lychgate Tea Rooms.

20 Great Hill and Roddlesworth

Great Hill is usually tackled from Brinscall and White Coppice to the west, but this circular route from Tockholes is the best in the whole of the West Pennines. It sees the finest sections of path in the woods of Roddlesworth before climbing the contrasting moors on the Great Hill's quiet side. It's a route for spring or early summer to see the colourful foliage and wild flowers.

Distance: 7 miles/11km	*followed by faint paths across fields north of Withnell Moor.*
Height gain: 850ft/260m	***Start/Finish:*** *Car park near the Royal Arms public house, Tockholes.*
Walking time: *4 hours*	
Type of walk: *Good paths through woodland, well-defined paths and tracks on Great Hill*	*GR665215*
	Map: *OS Explorer 19: West Pennine Moors.*

The walk starts in magnificent surroundings with the rich green woods of Roddlesworth filling the valley, contrasting with the bare brown slopes of Withnell Moor that rise above them. The woods and reservoirs of Roddlesworth are a haven for wildlife. Mallards and golden-eye frequent the lakes, while roe deer scuttle under the trees. Wild flowers include red campion, lesser celandine, golden saxifrage and wood sorrel in addition to a thick carpet of bluebells.

Go through the stile opposite the car park, taking the middle of three paths that descend into the woods. The prominent path descends south-west between low, crumbling walls through a wide avenue of trees and veers right across a small clearing. Ignore a left fork beyond the clearing, but follow the main path to the one-arched stone bridge over the River Roddlesworth. Do not cross the bridge but take the wide track, marked 'to Hollinshead Hall' and following the river's east bank. The track gradually rises above the riverbank, but at GR659207, a path forks right to return to it near some attractive waterfalls.

A short way beyond the falls, a concrete slab bridge allows the river to be crossed. The path now traces a subsidiary stream westwards to the busy A675 Belmont road at Calf Hey Bridge.

Across the road, the woods have been replaced by bare moors, capped by Great Hill, a small, rounded hump rising out of the surrounding pallid grasslands.

A stile allows access onto the moors, and a good path, bound by a fence and a crumbling wall, heads west through tussocky ground to follow the course of a small stream. The path gradually veers south before fording the stream just short of a stand of trees that surround the ruins of Pimms Farm. It makes a beeline for the top of Great Hill and is soon taking in its views.

Looking back across the Roddlesworth valley, Darwen Hill's stone-built Jubilee Tower juts into the sky above dark heathered hillslopes and the lush woods. To the

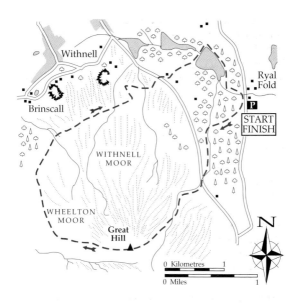

south, a wavy line of gritstone paving slabs traipses across the broad swell of moorland, leading the eye uneasily to the collection of masts and towers capping Winter Hill.

A well-defined path descends westwards on a grassy spur overlooking many a mile of dark heathland – Wheelton Moor to the north, Anglezarke Moor to the south.

Trees highlight the position of Great Hill Farm, but its green pastures are gradually fading in a return to the moors. A clump of trees and walls turning to rubble are all that remains of Drinkwaters. The farm numbered among the many that had to make way for the Anglezarke, Rivington and Yarrow reservoirs, which were completed in 1850 by the Liverpool Corporation.

The right of way shown as heading north across Brown Hill doesn't exist underfoot and it would be rough after periods of high rainfall. Stay with the stony track that develops after Drinkwaters. It parts company with the footpath to White Coppice by some steps and swings north-west across Heapy Moor, then north by a derelict wall.

Unfortunately, the Anglezarke and Rivington reservoirs are too deep-set to be in view, but the prospects are interesting. Towns and villages are scattered across the wide Lancashire plains to the west, while to the north the red bricked houses of Brinscall and the spired church of Withnell are surrounded by low pastured hills.

The stony track terminates at a gate by a metalled lane (GR632206). Once through the gate, turn right onto a pleasant farm track with one of those grassy islands. It aims north-east passing a ruined farmhouse before ending in a field. Two rutted farm tracks confuse the issue hereabouts. Ignore both of them but go half left, then follow a wall eastwards. There are no traces of the path on the ground.

Go through two tall gateposts (GR637209) and follow a path to the other side of the wall. The path is more dominant than the track shown on the Explorer map, and swings right to meet a heavily rutted vehicle track after 200yds/m. Here evidence of the continuing track disappears on rough pastureland, but maintain direction (east-north-east) to go through a gap in the next wall before descending boulder-studded ground to a stream crossing at GR643213. If in doubt, look out for the step-stile and wooden post in the fence beyond the track. They lie a short way to the south of some rubble heaps. (Note: Narrow sheep tracks on the ground from the wall go slightly north of the right of way before swinging right to the same point.)

Over the stile, the trackless route traverses fields east-north-east, passing the end of a rushy wall-lined track after 200yds/m. Here, follow the old wall on the right to the far end of the field where a rutted track leads the route north-west. At a stile by a gate turn right to follow a fence into a wooded dell south of some old quarries. The path crosses a bridge over the stream then climbs out to high fields where the fence leads to the busy Belmont road.

Across the road, the route now returns to the Roddlesworth valley. Go over the stile and across a field to a minor road by a farm. Turn right along the road, passing the farmhouse, then turn left on a metalled lane, which descends by a barn. At a padlocked gate, the path goes through a stone outhouse, using gates at both ends, before rejoining the lane and descending to the well-concealed dam of the upper reservoir.

Here the metalled lane veers right and a more rustic track, used on this route, descends further beneath the dam. A path climbs past the outflow on some steps to reach the northern shore, then rakes to the right on wooded slopes high above the reservoir. It joins another track along the upper edges of the wood before descending closer to the shores. Ignore the right fork, which will go down to the shore, but turn right a short way further on, on meeting a waymarked concessionary bridleway. This heads south across two small cloughs. Beyond the second, turn left to climb on a steep path that meets the road by the Royal Arms.

Donald Dakeyne

Winter Hill

21 Winter Hill

Endowed with an array of towers and masts, Winter Hill isn't everybody's idea of a country walk. It's a good viewpoint, however, and can be included in an enjoyable itinerary that takes in the attractive Longworth Clough, and an entertaining swoop down to Hordern Stoops and Belmont village.

Distance:
6 miles/10km
Height gain: 870 ft/266m
Walking time: 4 hours
Type of walk: Moderate walk on moorland paths and tracks. Steep drop off Winter Hill, which could be difficult in wintry conditions.
Start/Finish: Roadside lay-by at GR693157, east of Belmont.
Map: OS Explorer 19: West Pennine Moors.

The walk begins by the T-junction high on the hillside west of Delph Reservoir. Winter Hill dominates the scene across the valley, it's stark eastern slopes rising from the greenery of Longworth Clough. A well-defined grassy path descends south across fields from a roadside stile and into the depths of Longworth Clough. Beyond a second stile a narrow path weaves through bracken and bramble into oakwoods.

Some duckboards precede the crossing of the stream on a little wooden footbridge. Beyond the stream, the path veers half right, roughly following the banks before climbing west with woodland to the right. After crossing a stile in a fence, a clear route heads south-south-west, aiming for a cluster of cottages. It passes to the right of the cottages to join a farm track heading west to the Belmont road.

Turn right along the road towards the Wright's Arms but, just short of the pub, turn left towards Winter Hill on a track climbing just inside the boundaries of a pine plantation. At the top of the plantation, the path crosses a wide private road, then swings right, raking up Winter Hill's barren eastern slopes.

On reaching the brow of the hill, it's better not to enter the untidy complex of masts and towers. Instead, turn right to follow a narrow path by the fence perimeters. A stile allows access to the trig point for those who cannot resist the touch-the-top syndrome, though it's doubtful if the place is any higher.

On the northern fringes of the moor, the fence should be crossed to get to the route of descent. This begins very steeply down rocky eroded slopes, but eases on reaching a bouldery area. A stile here allows the path back to the east side of the fence.

(Note: I first used the above path when the slopes were crusted with ice and found it to be dangerous. In such conditions, descend further on the northern brow until the steep slopes relent, then double back, descending to meet the path by

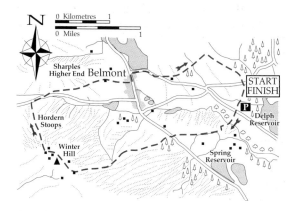

the aforementioned fence. Cross to the east side using one of the many stiles.)

Follow the fence northwards to the little road that straddles the moors between Belmont and Rivington then turn right towards Belmont. After a short way a grassy track on the left declines east across the sides of Sharples Higher End and beneath the crags that remain from old quarries.

Winter Hill's northern end, which more often than not will be hidden from the sun, appears as a satanic black dome when set against a bright afternoon sky.

A few trees shade the tumbledown cottage marked on current maps at GR669163. Over a step stile in the wall to the right, a well-defined path heads across fields towards the houses of Belmont. Take the right fork by the houses and follow an unsurfaced street to the main road.

Turn left down the road, then, after passing the last house, fork right on a little path down to the lane across Belmont Reservoir's dam. After passing a small copse of pine at the far side of the dam, the road should be abandoned for a signposted path (GR678164) leading east across the fields behind Higher Whittaker Farm. The path is unclear on the ground, but well-waymarked. Beyond the farm it passes to the left of another small pine plantation, marked on current Landranger maps, but not the OS Explorer.

Now the path runs along a raised embankment, veering north-east away from the perimeter fence. It descends into a deep, muddy clough, then out again, and crosses a stile in a fence before traversing the sombre lower slopes of Longworth Moor.

On reaching a footpath signpost at GR687167, where five paths meet, a heavily grooved track takes the route south-east past the pines and spruce of Moss Side Plantation. Where the track meets the road at a T-junction, go straight across, and head south to the start of the walk.

22 Cheetham Close and Turton Bottoms

The reservoirs of Turton and Entwistle, Wayoh and Jumbles may have devastated a wide area when constructed, but today they offer attractive walks round shores fringed by woodland and pasture. The reservoirs can be combined with a climb past historic Turton Tower to Cheetham Close where evidence of even older dwellings lies beneath the grass.

Distance: 5 miles/8km
Height gain: 650ft/200m
Walking time: 3 hours
Type of walk: Well-defined paths round the reservoir and in the valley, followed by a foolproof route across moorland.
Start/Finish: Car park, Turton and Entwistle Reservoir dam. GR723173
Map: OS Explorer 19: West Pennine Moors.

The walk begins on a good track from the south end of the bottom car park. It traces the top edge of woodland that fringes the narrow western finger of Wayoh Reservoir, and threads under one of the arches of a railway viaduct. Beyond the viaduct, the reservoir widens beneath extensive pastures and the hillslopes of Holcombe Moor.

Two church spires dominate views ahead. One towers over the three-storey terraces of Edgworth; the other,

Turton, stands proudly on hillsides to the right.

Cross the reservoir dam and turn right along a track into Edgworth, emerging at the roadside by the church and the Black Bull pub. The road descends, then curves right to cross the river at Turton Bottoms, passing en route another pub, the Spread Eagle.

Vale Street on the left takes the route between some renovated cottages before recrossing the river. Turn right along a signposted footpath along the east bank past several more cottages and into pleasant woodland. The meandering course leads to the shores of Jumbles Reservoir, where there is a sailing club.

A rather ugly concrete bridge takes the route to the west shores. Immediately opposite, the path leaves the reservoir and climbs the hillside on a stepped footpath to hilltop fields, where there are views back to the lake and across the rooftops of Bolton to the pale blue mist of Greater Manchester.

After passing a pond, the path descends to the B-road, 400yds/m south of Chapeltown. Turn left along the road then right, through the majestic gateposts of Turton Tower's grounds.

The wide metalled drive passes by the grand old fortified manor house. Although restored and modernised in Victorian times by James Kay, the pele tower was first constructed in the early-15th century. The fine timbered farmhouse dates back to the 16th century. Today Blackburn with Darwen

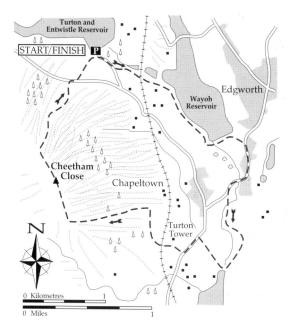

council care for the tower and ask visitors to consider the grounds as a conservation area.

Beyond the tower, a waterwheel, moved from its former position at Turton Bottoms, is being restored. The drive passes it before crossing a third curiosity. The bridge over the Manchester to Blackburn railway cutting has been constructed in ornate Norman fashion with mock towers and turrets.

Beyond the bridge a dirt track veers right (north) to climb to lofty fields, with Clough Farm visible in the mid-distance. The path to be taken at GR727155 is obscure in its beginnings. It coincides with a stile on the right, which is used by a right of way from a mill (also visible). Turn left uphill here, aiming for a barn high on the hillsides near some woods. After passing a pond near a whitewashed cottage on the right, the vague path climbs to a stile, left of the previously mentioned barn, then continues through the woodland and out on to the moor beyond a stile.

The path, vague again, roughly follows the line of a drystone wall on the left. On reaching the brow of the hill, go over the stile next to a gate in the fence, and head north-west on a clear dark path across the biscuit-coloured, tussocky moor.

A concrete trig point crowns the top, known as Cheetham Close. The views are wide, considering its modest 1,080ft/329m height. To the west, Belmont village nestles beneath Winter Hill, whose array of towers could be considered as the hilltop's crown of thorns. Only the limitations of the atmosphere stop the view continuing to the south of England, but generally Manchester, the Peak and Clwyd are plainly in sight.

Just north of the top are the obscure remains of two ancient stone circles, well worth seeking out for an exercise in detective work if nothing else. They are the remains of a Bronze Age village and burial mounds.

The path continues along the ridge, crossing a couple of stiles before coming to a concrete post marking the route down towards Entwistle. Turn right on a path that shows the string of reservoirs,

from Entwistle to Jumbles, beneath your
veers left to a stile in a wall beneath a line
pylons. Beyond the stile the path enters a tract of
wet, rushy moorland, but any difficulties are short-
lived. It then threads between two squat, grassy
knolls, one accompanied by a lone tree, before
descending to the groove of an old road.

Beyond the groove, a rushy track, bound by fences,
descends to the Greens Arms Road at its junction
with Clough House Farm's access track. Turn right
along the road for a few yards, then left on a
signposted footpath, descending across fields, back
to the car park.

Musbury Heights

The old weaving town of Helmshore lies at the western end of the busy Rossendale valley. Rising from the back yards of its mills and factories are Tor Hill and Musbury Heights. They can be combined in an interesting high level walk that discovers the remnants of bygone industries.

Distance:
6 miles/10km
Height gain:
740ft/225m
Walking time: 3 hours
Type of walk: Farm tracks and fairly easy paths across moorland.
Start/Finish: On B6214 road at Helmshore, close to the British Legion. GR781209
Map: OS Explorer 19: West Pennine Moors
Transport: Regular buses on a circular route from Haslingden and Rawtenstall stop at the British Legion, Helmshore.

The walk begins on a narrow metalled lane that climbs from opposite the British Legion to Tor End Farm, where it veers left. After scaling a dilapidated stile next to the cottage beyond the farm, follow a footpath climbing westwards across fields and guided by a drystone wall to the left.

By now there are fine views across Helmshore's rooftops to the surrounding hills of Rossendale. Straight ahead the squat gritstone-studded Tor Hill rises from the fields.

After a short distance, climb a ladder stile in the wall and head south-west on a path with a wall to the left. Just beyond the Great House Farm complex it joins a farm track, which rakes up the grassy southern flanks of Tor Hill. After passing to the right of a small sycamore plantation, the track terminates at a five-bar gate.

Beyond the gate, a well-defined path continues across moorland, dipping to the sombre but dramatic environs of the Musbury valley.

Here man has struggled and lost in his toils to tame the moors. The dark gritstone walls have crumbled and collapsed into the matt grass and rushes. High on the hillsides are the stark ruins of former farmsteads.

The path follows the course of derelict walls that round the head of this wild valley. The two streams forded en route are both confined by tight, craggy ravines in their upper regions.

The route, obvious underfoot, heads north, passing a substantial ruin (GR759205) before descending briefly to ford a side stream. Beyond the scant ruins of another old farmstead, the path encounters a curious rush-filled dyke. Be careful not to be lured onto a grooved path raking up the hillside hereabouts.

The dyke was constructed to form the boundary of the old 'Royal Deer Park', laid out in 1305 by Henry de Lacey, Earl of Lincoln. A fence of wooden palings ran along the raised ground next to the dyke.

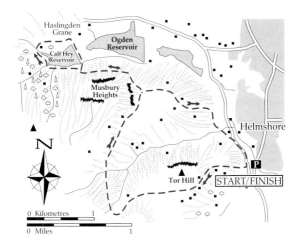

Beyond Rushy Leach, another ruin set in a marshy basin, the path veers to the right of the dyke and makes a bee-line for a gap stile in the wall at the edge of Musbury Heights' huge quarries. Take the left fork as the track divides a short distance further. This winds its way through mountainous spoil heaps to reach a wide quarry track to the east of an old chimney.

The chimney, which was part of an old engine house that powered the pulley-driven wagons, was in 1983 partially destroyed by lightning during a violent storm.

Turn right (north) at the chimney, past a spoil heap and pile of boulders, where a Rossendale Way sign (RW) points the way to the edge of the escarpment.

The path now looks down over the Haslingden Grane, a

wide valley filled by three large reservoirs – Calf Hey, Ogden and Holden Wood. They were constructed by the Bury Corporation Waterworks at the turn of the century. On the northern horizon, beyond the quarry-scarred Oswaldtwistle Moor, the bold whaleback escarpment of Pendle Hill nudges in front of the pale outlines of Ingleborough and Pen-y-Ghent.

The narrow path with frequent waymarking posts winds steeply downhill to join another one parallel to the lakeshore. Follow this westwards, crossing several stiles and footbridges over streams on an obvious waymarked course parallel with but well above the lakeshore.

By a post marked with the number six, a stony footpath veers north to cross a leat at the head of Calf Hey reservoir. Here it meets a wide track that should be followed beyond a large five-bar gate. The track veers left up hillslopes and traces the upper edge of a conifer plantation. It passes the preserved foundations of Hartley House, a 17th-century farmhouse (GR752226 and not named on OS maps).

Turn right through a kissing gate at the junction of tracks below the Calf Hey car park. The path now descends south to cross the reservoir's dam.

On the opposite side of the dam a narrow waymarked footpath climbs the hillside to reach the outward route at a wooden step-stile beneath a large sycamore tree.

To retrace the route as far as the chimney on

Musbury Heights, turn left parallel to the lakeshore, then right on a path (marked RW) beyond a stream crossing.

On reaching the chimney, the route heads east along a wide quarry track that was once an old tramway. Eventually, it rakes down the north-east slopes of the hill, curving to the right above two farmhouses to its termination by a five-bar gate (GR770217).

Through the gate, the route follows a farm track eastwards across lofty fields. After a short while, a footpath sign points to a path through a narrow avenue of shrubs and small trees. This leads to an unsurfaced country lane (GR776216). Turn right along it and descend past a large mill to reach the road at Helmshore just 100yds/m north of the starting point.

24 Boulsworth Hill and Foster's Leap

Boulsworth Hill, often known by the name of its summit, Lad Law, is one of the best viewpoints in Lancashire. Limitations of access mean that, at present, all approaches must be made from the north, either from Trawden or Wycoller. This figure-of-eight walk chooses the more interesting approach from Wycoller, a picturesque weavers' village with Brontë associations. It sets out to discover the weird gritstone rocks that ruffle the skyline, and takes in those wide vistas of Pendle and Yorkshire's Craven district.

Distance:
8 miles/13km
Walking time: 5 hours
Height gain:
1,200ft/400m
Type of walk: *A fairly strenuous walk across fields, on moorland paths and farm tracks. It has a stiff climb over rough,* wet moorland to Boulsworth Hill's summit.
Start/Finish: *Car park on the Laneshaw Bridge to Haworth road.* GR937393
Map: *OS Outdoor Leisure 21: South Pennines.*

The walk's first objective is Foster's Leap, a couple of huge gritstone outcrops to the east. Although it is possible to get to them using field paths, it is much quicker to start along the road, which, has great views of Boulsworth Hill and Wycoller Dene.

Leave the road after 400yds/m for an access track on the right, which descends beneath the Foster's Leap rocks.

It is reputed that Foster Cunliffe, whose family lived at nearby Wycoller Hall, leaped safely from one of the rocks to the other. In a separate incident, a suspected thief was offered freedom if he could do the same. The thief, on horseback, safely negotiated the gap but neither horse nor rider could stop in time and fell to their deaths.

The track continues beneath the rocks to Foster's Leap Farm. Circumvent the farm to the north and west, then follow a concessionary short-cut south through a gate by the side of the old house. The path now descends south-east across fields into the depths of Wycoller Dene. A gate at the end of the bottom field allows access to a footbridge across Wycoller Beck by Parson Lee Farm.

Turn left on an unsurfaced lane, climbing to lofty pastures that are shaded by the barren moorland slopes of Dove Stones Moor. The track ends at a T-junction with an old packhorse route skirting the moorland. Turn right, then take the right fork, a rushy track heading south-west beneath the farmhouse at Brink Ends and down to ford the stream in Turnhole Clough. The old packhorse route climbs south out of the clough, veering south-west under Broadhead Moor. It becomes intermittently paved with slabs of millstone grit that appear to be sinking into the rushy terrain.

To the right are high pastures declining to Trawden: to the left, beyond the hollow of Saucer Hill Clough, the

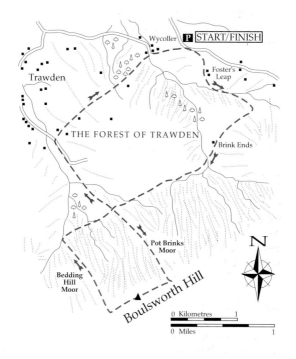

The following labels appear on the map:

Wycoller **P** START/FINISH

Foster's Leap

Trawden

THE FOREST OF TRAWDEN

Brink Ends

Pot Brinks Moor

Bedding Hill Moor

▲ Boulsworth Hill

N

0 Kilometres 1

0 Miles 1

rough pallid course grasses rise to the serrated profiles of the Great Saucer Stones.

The ascent of Boulsworth Hill, a North West Water courtesy route, begins by the lonely farm of Spoutley Lumb on a concrete road climbing south-east to a small reservoir. From here, a waymarked path rises steeply on the concave peaty slopes of Pot Brinks Moor. A few small gritstone outcrops (The Little Chair Stones) come into view on gaining the ridge.

The ensuing route across the wide peaty ridge climbs easily to the Weather Stones, an impressive group of weirdly eroded crags whose nooks and crannies offer good shelter against the elements. Boulsworth Hill's summit, Lad Law, lies a little to the west, marked by a concrete trig point set close to more gritstone crags.

Some say the place has a sinister past. The name has its origins in the Celtic word 'Llad', meaning slaughter and 'Law' meaning hill. They conclude from this that here was a Druid altar of sacrifice. More pragmatic historians believe that the rock is no more than an old boundary stone, eroded by time and the harsh elements.

Whatever its past, the summit gives striking views over the industrial towns of Colne, Nelson and Burnley to the whaleback of Pendle Hill and, further afield, to Bowland, Pen-y-Ghent, Ingleborough and the Lakeland fells.

The descent begins on a well-defined path across Bedding Hill Moor. It returns to the old packhorse route used earlier, only this time, a little further to the west. Turn right and follow the track back to a ladder stile beyond Spoutley Lumb Farm. Over the stile, the line of the wall on the left sets the direction for a descent across fields. It veers very slightly right through a grassy depression to reach a concrete bridge over a stream.

A short detour to the left leads to Lumb Spout, a pleasant waterfall cascading over a sandstone cliff into a hollow of oak, ash and rowan. The falls are almost certainly man-made for the course of the river has been diverted to the top of the cliffs.

Return to the bridge, where the route continues north-west across fields, passing to the right of a farm (Lodge Moss) before meeting a narrow country lane. Follow this downhill to a large mill at Hollin Hall, south of Trawden.

Take the track signposted 'to Wycoller and Raven's Rock' at the far end of the mill. It climbs across pastures and turns sharp left towards Far Wanless Farm. Leave it here and cross the dilapidated stile for a path bearing half-right (east) by a wall. After passing Little Laithe Farm, the route continues east by the wall, passing to the left of Germany Farm and Raven's Rock Farm, crossing several primitive stiles and a couple of dykes en route.

Beyond Raven's Rock Farm, the path descends through a young plantation of larch, birch, rowan and alder. It meets a stony farm track, which descends into Wycoller village where the visitor is transported into a 17th-century scene with

Wycoller and its bridges

picturesque weavers' cottages huddled into a narrow verdant vale.

Wycoller once thrived on the exploits of both farming and weaving. On the decline of those industries it was purchased by the water authorities who had intended to construct a reservoir here, but never implemented the scheme. In 1973, Lancashire County Council bought much of the area and turned it into the delightful country park it is today.

Wycoller Hall, now in ruins, was built in the 16th century as a country house for the wealthy Cunliffe family. The last squire, spendthrift Henry Cunliffe, built up debts. On his death in 1774, the estate was divided and sold to repay them and the hall was left to decay. It would have been empty in the time of Charlotte Brontë but the location inspired Fearndean Manor in her book, Jane Eyre.

The fine twin-arched packhorse bridge across Wycoller Beck has origins in the 13th century, but there are two more unusual bridges to the south through the village. The Clapper Bridge, opposite the ruins of Wycoller Hall, consists of three slabs of stone spanning two piers. The more austere Clam Bridge, a single slab of gritstone, is reputed to be more than a thousand years old. It has had a hard time of late, being swept off its perch after flash floods in 1989 and 1991.

A cup of tea and a scone at the cafe is perhaps called for, before climbing the stepped that climbs out of the dene by Wycoller Hall back to the car park and the start of the walk.

25 Black Hameldon

At Black Hameldon, the border between Lancashire and Yorkshire runs along one of the South Pennine's wettest ridges – sounds inviting, doesn't it? Well, there's drama here; there are powerfully sculpted dark rocks looking down on sombre, remote, man-made pools, and there are graceful hillslopes that bring to mind the stark romance of a Brontë novel.

Distance: 7¹/₂ miles/12km
Height gain: 950ft/290m
Walking time: 4¹/₂ hours
Type of walk: A fairly strenuous walk across wet moorland. Compass and map skills are essential.
Start/Finish: Car Park, Hurstwood. GR882313
Map: OS Outdoor Leisure 21: South Pennines.

It's worth having a look at Hurstwood before setting out for the hills, for there are several fine 16th-century buildings, including Hurstwood Hall, Tattersall's House and Spenser's cottage. The last-mentioned was home to 16th-century poet Edmund Spenser whose works include The Faerie Queen.

From the car park, the route heads north-east towards Hurstwood Reservoir along a road lined by an avenue of pine, larch, beech and rhododendron. Just before the dam an arrow highlights a narrow path on the right, threading through the trees to meet the Cant Clough reservoir track at GR889314. The stony road climbs through disused quarries to the dam of Cant Clough Reservoir, which lies beneath the grassy flanks of Worsthorne Moor.

From the dam, follow a track along the northern shoreline, then leave it for a waymarked path climbing towards the wide col between Gorple Stones and Black Hameldon. The col's gritstone outcrops, known as Hare Stones, jut out on the skyline and act as a guide in clear conditions.

In the upper reaches the terrain is tougher, and the sketchy path traverses, first, tussocky moorland, then, beyond Rams Clough at GR908315, a rush-covered marshy area.

The Hare Stones offer shelter from the winds that can howl across the col. As such, they make a useful refreshment stop, for Hoof Stones Height does not have any shelter. To the east, across your coffee cup, the wild dark hollow cradling the Gorple Reservoirs, can then be studied in relative comfort.

From Hare Stones, the path climbs on Black Hameldon's peat-scarred slopes to gain the long broad ridge that spans a mile or so to Hoof Stones Height. From the summit trig point, which is surrounded by peaty pools, the hills of Derbyshire, West Lancashire and the Craven area parade themselves across the horizon.

There are no paths southwards off Black Ham-

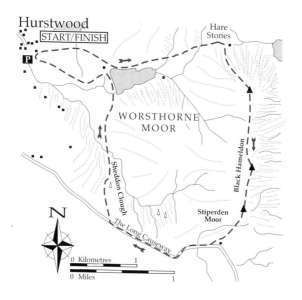

eldon. A recent permissive route heads east, but that's Yorkshire! Instead, head south-west across trackless grassy slopes to the Long Causeway, a high metalled lane that once was a packhorse route between Burnley and Halifax.

Thirsty walkers could detour to the Sportsman's Arms, about 1½ miles/2km to the east, but otherwise turn right and follow the lane to the car park south of Sheddon Clough and opposite Coal Clough wind farm.

From the back of the car park, follow a stony path heading north across the moors before descending through trees to Sheddon Clough, where grassy mounds are interspersed with rhododendron.

The disturbances are the remnants of man-made limestone hushings. Limestone from the Yorkshire Dales, deposited here by glaciers in the last ice-age, was valuable, not only for building mortar, but to 'sweeten' or neutralise the acidity of the farmland. To discover and separate the limestone, dykes, which were dug from the top of the hill, were dammed to create ponds. The dams were then breached, causing the water to gush downhill, removing the topsoil, and thereby revealing any limestone.

In the early stages the route follows the red and yellow Burnley Way signs along the prominent, wall-enclosed track in the clough bottom. It stays with the Burnley Way to veer right, encircling a particularly bouldery area. At GR894299, the Burnley Way slants off to the left to rejoin the main track and should be abandoned for a narrow but well-defined path climbing the grassy mound ahead (north). The path soon comes upon a wide dirt track climbing back to the grassy dam of Cant Clough Reservoir, where it meets the outward route on the northern side. Retrace earlier steps across the old quarries through the woods, then turn left along the track back to the car park.

Other Dalesman titles for walkers

Walking and Trail Guides

LAKE DISTRICT, WESTERN FELLS Paddy Dillon £5.99
LAKE DISTRICT, EASTERN FELLS Paddy Dillon £5.99
WHITE PEAK Martin Smith £4.99
DARK PEAK John Gillham £4.99
NORTH PENNINES Alan Hall £4.99
SOUTH PENNINES John Gillham £4.99
CLEVELAND WAY Martin Collins £4.99
PENNINE WAY Terry Marsh £4.99

Walks Around Series: Peak District

BAKEWELL Martin Smith £1.99
BUXTON Andrew McCloy £1.99
CASTLETON John Gillham £1.99
MATLOCK Martin Smith £1.99

Walks Around Series: Lake District

AMBLESIDE Tom Bowker £1.99
HAWKSHEAD Mary Welsh £1.99
KESWICK Dawn Gibson £1.99
WINDERMERE Robert Gambles £1.99

Pub and Tea Shop Walks Series

LAKE DISTRICT Terry Marsh £5.99
NORTH YORK MOORS & COAST Richard Musgrave £5.99
PEAK DISTRICT John Morrison £5.99
YORKSHIRE DALES Richard Musgrave £5.95

Safety for Walkers

MOUNTAIN SAFETY Kevin Walker £4.99
MAP READING Robert Matkin £3.50

Available from all good bookshops. In case of difficulty contact
Dalesman Publishing Company, Clapham Via Lancaster
LA2 8EB. Tel: 015242 51225